WASHINGTON, *in the Territory of* COLUMBIA.

A PREMIUM

OF FIVE HUNDRED DOLLARS, or a MEDAL of that value, at the option of the party, will be given by the Commissioners of the Federal Buildings, to the person who, before the fifteenth day of July next, shall produce to them the most approved PLAN, if adopted by them, for a PRESIDENT's HOUSE, to be erected in this City. The size of the building, if the artist will attend to it, will of course influence the aspect and outline of his plan; and it's destination will point out to him the number, size, and distribution of the apartments. It will be a recommendation of any plan, if the central part of it may be detached and erected for the present, with the appearance of a complete whole, and be capable of admitting the additional parts, in future, if they shall be wanting. Drawings will be expected of the ground plats, elevations of each front, and sections through the building, in such directions as may be necessary to explain the internal structure; and an estimate of the cubic feet of brick-work composing the whole mass of the walls.

March 14, 1792.   *tf*   THE COMMISSIONERS.

STEPHEN ALCORN	KEVIN HAWKES	RICHARD PECK
GIGI AMATEAU	HOMER HICKAM	STEPHANIE TRUE PETERS
M. T. ANDERSON	LEE BENNETT HOPKINS	MATT PHELAN
JENNIFER ARMSTRONG	POLLY HORVATH	JERRY PINKNEY
JEANNINE ATKINS	BAGRAM IBATOULLINE	TOM POHRT
TONY AUTH	PAUL B. JANECZKO	DON POWERS
NATALIE BABBITT	STEVE JOHNSON	JACK PRELUTSKY
MARY BRIGID BARRETT	STÉPHANE JORISCH	JAMES RANSOME
SOPHIE BLACKALL	STEVEN KELLOGG	CHRIS RASCHKA
JESS M. BRALLIER	BARBARA KERLEY	MIKE REAGAN
CALEF BROWN	RALPH KETCHAM	LYNDA JOHNSON ROBB
DON BROWN	ELIZABETH CODY KIMMEL	BARRY ROOT
JOSEPH BRUCHAC	BOB KOLAR	S. D. SCHINDLER
ROBERT BYRD	KATHLEEN KRULL	JON SCIESZKA
MEG CABOT	JIM LaMARCHE	BRIAN SELZNICK
ERIC CARLE	STEPHANIE LOER	CHRIS SHEBAN
NANCY CARPENTER	WILLIAM LOW	ANITA SILVEY
JOE CEPEDA	P.J. LYNCH	PETER SÍS
R. GREGORY CHRISTIE	DAVID MACAULAY	DAVID SLONIM
JOHN Y. COLE	PATRICIA MacLACHLAN	DAVID SMALL
MICHAEL COOPER	GREGORY MAGUIRE	JERRY SPINELLI
SUSAN COOPER	LEONARD S. MARCUS	SARAH STEWART
MARGUERITE W. DAVOL	ALBERT MARRIN	MATT TAVARES
KATE DiCAMILLO	PETRA MATHERS	MARK TEAGUE
DIANE DILLON	DAVID McCULLOUGH	STEPHANIE S. TOLAN
LEO DILLON	EMILY ARNOLD McCULLY	CHRIS VAN DUSEN
CAROL DYER	MEGAN McDONALD	DIANA WALKER
JANE DYER	FREDRICK L. McKISSACK	ANDRÉA WESSON
TIMOTHY BASIL ERING	PATRICIA C. McKISSACK	TERRY WIDENER
LOU FANCHER	MILTON MELTZER	NANCY WILLARD
RUSSELL FREEDMAN	WENDELL MINOR	MARK LONDON WILLIAMS
TONY FUCILE	BARRY MOSER	MICHAEL WINERIP
JEAN CRAIGHEAD GEORGE	ROXIE MUNRO	VIRGINIA EUWER WOLFF
LEONID GORE	WALTER DEAN MYERS	JANE YOLEN
MAX GRAFE	CLAIRE NIVOLA	ED YOUNG
BARBARA HARRISON	LINDA SUE PARK	JAMES YOUNG, M.D.
	KATHERINE PATERSON	

OUR WHITE HOUSE

LOOKING IN, LOOKING OUT

CREATED BY 108 RENOWNED AUTHORS AND ILLUSTRATORS
AND THE NATIONAL CHILDREN'S BOOK AND LITERACY ALLIANCE

WITH AN INTRODUCTION BY DAVID MCCULLOUGH

CANDLEWICK PRESS
CAMBRIDGE, MASSACHUSETTS

Compilation copyright © 2008 by the National Children's Book and Literacy Alliance

Copyright acknowledgments as well as credit lines for public domain material appear on page 232.

Frontispiece illustration: detail from pages xiv–1, copyright © 2008 by Bagram Ibatoulline

First edition 2008

Library of Congress Cataloging-in-Publication Data is available.

Library of Congress Catalog Card Number 2007943581

ISBN 978-0-7636-2067-7

2 4 6 8 10 9 7 5 3 1

Printed in the United States of America

This book was typeset in Adobe Caslon.

Candlewick Press
2067 Massachusetts Avenue
Cambridge, Massachusetts 02140

visit us at www.candlewick.com

Dedicated to young people everywhere
— The NCBLA

ACKNOWLEDGMENTS

The National Children's Book and Literacy Alliance thanks the Office of First Lady Laura Bush for their assistance. We are grateful for the grant given by the Verizon Foundation that allowed us to launch this historic project. We extend our deepest appreciation to historian David McCullough and all the gifted writers and illustrators who have donated their time and talent to this effort. The following institutions have provided invaluable help and assistance: the Center for the Book at the Library of Congress; the American Antiquarian Society; the City Museum of Washington, D.C.; the George Washington University Gelman Library; and the Paterson Family Foundation. This book would not have been possible without the generous support and publishing expertise of Candlewick Press. Last but not least, the NCBLA would like to thank the young people for and with whom we have worked, whose questions and concerns have shaped *Our White House*, especially the students at East Elementary Alternative School in Sharon, Massachusetts.

All royalties from *Our White House* will go directly to the NCBLA, a not-for-profit organization of young people's authors and illustrators that educates and advocates for literacy, literature, libraries, and the arts. The NCBLA has created a companion website for *Our White House* at www.ourwhitehouse.org, which includes resources to expand young people's knowledge of American history. To learn more about the NCBLA, and to find many great ideas and projects that will help kids become great readers and writers, go to www.thencbla.org.

The Board of the National Children's Book and Literacy Alliance and Candlewick Press
would like to extend a special thank-you to Mary Brigid Barrett for initiating the idea for this book,
as well as for being its indefatigable editor in chief and contributing immeasurably to the
creative force that helped bring this diverse, comprehensive volume together.

CONTENTS

INTRODUCTION BY DAVID McCULLOUGH

Our presidents have come in all shapes and sizes, from all kinds of backgrounds and places near and far. They've been tall, short, fat, skinny, farmers, soldiers, lawyers, and presidents of colleges. One was a tailor before taking up politics, another a world-famous engineer, another a movie star. Seven came from Ohio, two from Texas, one from Missouri, one from Georgia, another from Arkansas. The tallest, as you would expect, was Abraham Lincoln of Illinois. He was six feet four. The smallest, James Madison of Virginia, stood just over five feet and weighed 100 pounds at most. William Howard Taft, on the other hand, weighed at least three times that, at more than 330 pounds!

They had all kinds of interests as well. Thomas Jefferson played the violin. John Quincy Adams wrote poetry. Franklin Roosevelt was a stamp collector. General Eisenhower liked to paint. Some were rich, some poor. Calvin Coolidge said as little as possible; Theodore Roosevelt rarely ever stopped talking.

But different as they were, they all, every one, starting with John Adams in 1800, lived in the White House, along with wives, children, grandchildren, in-laws, servants, countless overnight guests, and no end of dogs, cats, birds—and mice. Once, at a meeting with a presidential assistant in his tiny West Wing office, I noticed on the floor by the corner of his desk what looked very much like an everyday mousetrap complete with a bit of yellow cheese. "Is that what it looks like?" I asked. "Yes, indeed," he said, adding something to the effect that while presidents come and go, mice at the White House reside in perpetuity.

And so do ghosts, according to President Harry Truman, as he wrote to his wife, Bess, late one night in his upstairs study:

> *I sit here in this old house and work on foreign affairs, read reports, and work on speeches—all the while listening to the ghosts walk up and down the hallway and even right here in the study. The floors pop and the drapes move back and forth—*

I can just imagine old Andy and Teddy having an argument over Franklin. Or James Buchanan and Franklin Pierce deciding which was the more useless to the country. And when Millard Fillmore and Chester Arthur join in for place and show the din is almost unbearable. . . .

Truman could feel the presence of his predecessors because he knew the history of the presidency and of the White House about as well as anyone who ever lived there. Though he was the only president of the twentieth century who never went to college, his love of history had started early, inspired by a favorite teacher in high school, Margaret Phelps, who knew history to be essential to learning, as she affirmed in a memorable statement of faith. History, she wrote, "cultivates every faculty of the mind, enlarges sympathies, liberalizes thought and feeling, furnishes and approves the highest standards of character."

The White House is the most important, the most famous, the most historic, the most beloved house in all the land, and it is filled with—no, overflowing with—stories . . . stories reflecting and embodying the drama of mighty historic events without, and of altogether human stories within. It has been the focal point of great moments of national celebration as well as overwhelming sorrow. It has been the scene of weddings, state banquets, and grand balls, when music played into the night. Presidents and the beloved of presidents have breathed their last breaths within its walls. Children have been born there. Ideas have been born there. Momentous decisions wise and foolish have been made there. Indeed, little there is in the infinite range of human experience that has not happened there. But then, that is what history is—human—and that is why we can never know enough about it.

What a splendid thing it is that so charming and lively a book as this captures so much of the story of the White House. Let us hope it will be read and enjoyed far and wide for a very long time to come. It is our White House, after all. It is our story, after all.

Looking In, Looking Out

Gregory Maguire

A few steamy acres upwind of the malarial Potomac, a great House grows. Foundations are dug, plumb lines strung, stones set, windows framed, rafters raised, walls plastered. Not a single inch of it is incidental. Well, it's easy to govern a house. Houses are a lot of lines ruled by strict geometry.

Domestic architecture follows its own laws of pressure and resistance. Laws of gravity. And houses obey the laws of time. (Paint flakes. Plaster develops stress fractures. Wood warps.)

The White House is as correct as any other big house of its period. It conforms to expectation with a persnickety crispness of angles. The front door is impeccably central. To the eighth-inch, pilasters are the same width. At regulated intervals, tall windows blink through its facades, and though the pediment styles vary—shallow curved eyebrows, shallow triangles—the arrangement of them, from each of the building's corners, is symmetrical.

However, as for the trees, gardens, the world around the house—just think of the tendency of vines to trail, of hedges to poke and seethe in new growth. Of lawns to go to seed, given half a chance. The world outside the windows of any house has a habit of breaking free. One might as well try to govern the shape and spacing of the clouds in the sky.

Let's look in, for a century or two, at the White House. (Come on; we have the right. It's our house too.) Those who live in the house, for a few years or for many, see home improvements, redecorations from salon to parlor, renovations and restorations from basement to rooftop.

And let's look out, too. Out of the windows, into the world. Residents and visitors alike see another set of rules at work: not of geometry, but of history. Herewith, a history as it involves human progress and potential, human despair—and human hope.

There are as many ways to tell a story as there are voices to try. There are as many views, looking in and out of the White House windows, as there are eyes to look.

ILLUSTRATION BY
Bagram Ibatoulline

PART I

From the Foundation Up

The White House First Residents

An Imagined Conversation Between John and Abigail Adams

* * * * * * * * * *

JANE YOLEN

illustrated by PETRA MATHERS

Dearest John, the House is large.
The rooms are many; I have been lost.

Dearest Abigail, it's not a home.
It's far too grand; I count the cost.

Dearest John, the cost was great,
But count instead the folks who see
The grandness of the President's House,
Not small like you, dear John, or me.

Dearest Abigail, the architect
Was Irish born, not from our shores.

Dearest John, our shores are wide;
The House has many open doors.

Dearest Abigail, all I see is
Staircase, rooms still incomplete,
Without good carpets on the floors;
I hear the sounds of many feet.

Dearest John, the many feet
Belong to people good and true,
The honest, energetic, kind,
The ones who gave their vote to you.

Dearest Abigail, the wash
That's hanging from the clothing line
Strung up along the East Room wall
Does not, I fear, look very fine.

Dearest John, that wash is dry
And taken down, but all agree,
Since here there is no laundry yard,
They'd rather see than smell dear thee.

Dearest Abigail, you're right;
You always see the straight way through.

Dearest John, of course I am,
Because I married well — to you.

TESTIMONY OF
PADRAIG TOMÁS Ó'DEORÁIN
1801

memoir imagined and illustrated by

Mary Brigid Barrett

I CAME TO THE HOUSE apprentice to my father. Washington City, we'd read, was a dreary hamlet seething with malaria, full of rooting pigs, marauding dogs, and noxious reptiles of enormous size—but come we did, the two of us. James Hoban had writ in need of my father's skills; with my dear *máthair* dead, there was naught to hold us in Dublin. We packed our tools and essentials and set sail on the first ship out of Liverpool. We looked to a brighter future in America.

Disembarking, we found New York a bustling metropolis. Local builders wooed us with lucrative offers and pints of good ale. We were tempted to stay and work, for skilled craftsmen were in great demand. But wasn't Mr. Hoban an old friend of my father's from Kilkenny and his need even greater? And so, through villages small and forests thick, we journeyed on.

Isn't it a wonder, I said to my father, that President Washington himself should take notice of the likes of James Hoban, summoning him to Philadelphia to discuss the architectural competition for the president's house? James Hoban, whose work in Dublin years back had earned him no great reputation for either imaginative design or innovative construction!

'Tis not Christian to spit on a man's good fortune, my father reminded me, tweaking my queue. Indeed, he added, good fortune is of a certainty James Hoban's lot, for who else in the competition had been afforded a personal tour of the building site in ample time of the contest's deadline? Who else had been shown artist L'Enfant's original sketches for the presidential palace? Plans that had pleased the president but not the famous Mr. Jefferson, whose political inclinations dictated a house of much smaller size. Surely, my father said with a wink and a smile, it had to be blessed good fortune, and not presidential favoritism, that favored his old friend James Hoban above all other competitors?

He reached into his waistcoat pocket and drew out Mr. Hoban's letter, containing the tattered competition advertisement Mr. Jefferson had composed for the newspapers. It demanded an estimate of the cubic feet of brick needed to build the house's walls. The truth of it was, James Hoban confided in his letter, that the president wanted a house of stone, with sufficient decorative carving to lend it an air of elegance. Stone carvers were scarce in America. Upon winning the competition, Mr. Hoban sent to Dublin quick for my father. Come to Washington City, he wrote. Help me to build a house for the president.

Our feet blistered, we arrived at the District of Columbia, finding not a city at all but a vast expanse of country, part wilderness, part fields of wheat, corn, and orchard, dotted here and there by a lone house or barn. The site for the president's house sat on a rise looking out over a stream onto streaks of green marshland. Goose Creek the stream is called by some, but others call it the Tiber, James Hoban informed us after a warm welcome, showing us the lay of the land. He said a man named Pope had originally owned a portion of the acreage. With his land bordering the Tiber, he called his plantation Rome. And why not, said my father, for isn't every man entitled to his dreams?

The north yard was riddled with workers' shacks and sheds, tempering pits, kilns, piles of brick, stacks of lumber, a cookhouse, a sawmill, a carpenter's hall, and a lodge for the masons. Mules brayed, chickens squawked, and indeed a stray hog or two could be seen rooting about in the muck. Mean and surly those hogs can be, boyo, James Hoban warned me. Best to keep a stick about you at night if you go wandering. He pointed to stacks of freestone, piled high. Each block had been marked at the quarry according to Hoban's plans, then brought to the site to be assembled like a giant puzzle. My father inspected the gray sandstone. This stone is porous, he said. Will it not freeze and crack? Sure and it will, said James Hoban. We will have to seal it with a strong limewash of white to keep the wet from seeping in. We had arrived at a fortuitous moment. Built by slaves, the house's foundation was finished; the brick inner walls, two feet thick, were most complete. It was indeed time for the stone walls to rise.

James Hoban left us, called away to settle a dispute, and we inspected the stonecutters' shed. A barrel-chested man with massive forearms swaggered over and introduced himself as Collen Williamson, a Scot and master stonemason. His surly manner made clear his disdain for Irishmen. In front of his masons, Edinburgh men all, Williamson challenged my father, insisting he prove his skills. Selecting a block of stone the size of a grave marker, he hoisted it onto a banker's table and spat, hitting his target—my father's shoes.

Chatter ceased, and the men waited, and Williamson waited, to see what my father would do. But I knew my da was not one to be intimidated. Tall and ramrod straight, he approached the stone with a knowing eye, an experienced hand, and a silent tongue; he would not waste one word on the brute. Quickly, I removed his tools from our rucksack—chisels, hammers, rasps, rifflers—tools that my grandfather had used, and his father before him, and set them on the table. Closing his eyes, my father slowly ran his long, tapered fingers along the stone's edges, touching every inch of its unforgiving surface. Without hesitation, with no sketch beside him, he began to carve. He worked swiftly and surely, the stone falling away chip by chip, as if he were merely marking butter with a knife. Hours passed like minutes. From his hands a flower grew, not a predictable cabbage rose, but a delicate Irish rose, its petals and leaves fluttering in an imagined wind.

There being now no question of my father's abilities, Williamson reluctantly withdrew. My father was given his own place in the shed to work; I was to serve as his assistant. He began the intricate carving for the north facade of the president's house. President Washington himself visited the building site and was impressed with my father's work. He insisted that my father plan the carvings over the north portal; my father sketched a swag of roses and oak leaves to be placed over the door. Increasingly, James Hoban took my father into his confidence. In his sketch for the front pediment, James Hoban had drawn a great eagle, its wings spread wide, a carving he would now entrust to my father. Hoban added an entablature plaque to the front facade, centered below the pediment. He asked my father to create a sketch for the plaque to submit for the president's approval. My father was honored by the request.

The days passed quickly—toiling, moiling, hauling, lifting, with nary a break from red dawn 'til dewy dusk. Sunday provided our only day of rest, with morning Mass at Saint Patrick's, afternoon fishing on the Tiber. Diligently I worked by my father's side, preparing the stone, executing simple carvings. And didn't my skills improve and my fist grow strong? My father took notice and gave me more detailed work to carve. He took me with him when he met with President Washington and Mr. Hoban to show them his sketches for the entablature. A tall, grand man was the president, with a head of white hair, though teeth false and brown made his breath a bit sour. The president admired my father's sketches. He was well pleased with the work my father had completed.

Weeks sped by, and the walls grew tall. My father finished the swag of oak leaves and was half finished with the inner arch of acanthus. I made a substantial contribution to the effort, for my skills at carving leaves and florals had improved. My father was nearing the apex on the right side of the surround arch. Suddenly he stood up. He threw down his chisel, requesting paper and graphite.

He asked, did not the entrance arch deserve a pair of valiant gatekeepers? He sketched with zest, and I watched, fascinated, as his dark lines took shape, becoming great griffins with the bodies of lions, the wings, heads, and talons of eagles. Griffins, he said, pulled the chariot of the god Apollo. Alexander the Great was said to have ridden on the backs of griffins to the edge of the sky. Griffins represent wisdom joined to fortitude, my father stated, with wisdom always in the lead.

Through oppressive heat and humidity he worked, finishing most of the first griffin by day's end. Of necessity, the stonemasons had drunk a great deal of ale and whiskey, especially those who worked high on the walls—the higher up a mason worked, the more whiskey he was allotted. My father was himself drenched in sweat. He sent me to fetch him a mug of ale, but I was curious to see how work on the walls progressed and stopped to look at the men turning the treadmill, hoisting a stone block high in the air, maneuvering it into its place on the wall. I heard my father's call. I turned, watching him amble toward me from the shed. I knew I was in for a bit of a scold, having failed to return promptly with his drink, but it would be a light chiding, for he had an amused smile on his face; he knew too well my fascination with all aspects of construction. Neither of us heard the cable on the treadmill snap. I watched, unbelieving and helpless as the stone block fell through the air, fell full upon my father, crushing his chest.

James Hoban helped me arrange for my father's funeral and his burial in consecrated ground. There were no women to cry and keen for him, and so through the dark night I crept down to the river and in the reeds hid, mourning my father and my *máthair* and all who had gone before me, my tears swallowed by the river and the black sky above. Too soon my father had been taken. I could not leave his work undone.

Most all the Scots had come to admire and respect my father, but one mason, Austin McGinty, coveted my father's position—bitter and jealous he was. As Collen Williamson had tested my father, McGinty now challenged me and my right to finish my father's work. Men filled the shed; the air was thick with the stink of their sweat. Every eye fell upon me as I plunked a stone slab onto the table. One by one I laid out my father's tools. I felt the width and the breadth of the stone, skimming every inch of its skin. And as I spread my hands wide across its cold surface, I saw, for the first time, that my hands were shaped very like my father's. I began to carve, petal by petal, leaf by leaf, coaxing a fair rose out from the stone. One of the watching masons stepped past McGinty to inspect my work and declared, Aye, he has his father's fist.

Then didn't I spend every waking moment working? To the best of my limited abilities, I mirrored my father's work, sculpting the left side of the surround. I saved the griffin for the last, giving all my heart to the effort. I knew I could not achieve the master quality of my father's work; there is a marked difference betwixt the beasts, my father's griffin being by far the better. Despite my deficiencies, James Hoban and the president were well pleased. I realized the intricate work my father had planned for the entablature and the pediment were beyond my skills, and as no other mason present could sculpt the stone with my father's artistry, those carvings were abandoned.

My father's work complete, I was determined to see it placed, and so, with the masons, I climbed the scaffolding, angling the surround arch into its proper position above the door. Austin McGinty wedged the piece into place. Suddenly it jerked. My right hand

caught between the stones, mangling my fingers. Though naught could be proved against McGinty, the other masons shunned him. The dirty lout drank more and more, and one Sunday he trailed a group of men to Baltimore. He was not among them when they returned at curfew.

The masonry work was complete. Most of the carvers returned to Scotland, though a few stayed to work on the Capitol building. My hand healed but had not the strength to work in stone. I found I had a talent, and a liking, for plastering and carpentry so chose to stay and work on at the mansion. And wasn't it there, in the house, that I felt most my father's presence?

Weeks and months passed quickly as we prepared for President Adams and the government's move from Philadelphia to Washington City. The first of November, 1800, came too soon. The president arrived, finding no yard, fence, walkway, or well. Inside, closet doors went missing. Windows rattled in the wind. Wet walls reeked sour. The main staircase was still but a few inked lines on James Hoban's house plans, its location a gaping hole in the floor. Furniture was scattered about, scarred and damaged after shipment from Philadelphia. The only ornament worthy of the mansion was a framed portrait of President Washington, which Head Carpenter Middleton and I screwed onto the wall of the levee room. But I had cleaned the outhouse and stoked the fires in thirty-nine hearths. The commissioners officially welcomed John Adams to the new president's house; the warmth from my fires welcomed him home.

My father believed that artists leave a piece of their soul in their work, giving it life. To be sure, my father gave the best that was within him to this whitewashed house. It is his griffins that guard and protect all who reside here. And to those who walk beneath the griffins' wings, I can only echo the blessings and the wish that our president, John Adams, shared with me the morning he first woke in this house, a prayer he set down in a letter to his wife, Abigail, bidding her to join him—

I pray Heaven to bestow the best of Blessings on this House
and all that shall hereafter inhabit it.
May none but honest and wise Men ever rule under this roof.

SLAVES HELPED BUILD THE WHITE HOUSE!

Walter Dean Myers

THE HEADLINES SUGGESTED AN OUTRAGE. Why wasn't it common knowledge that some of the laborers who built the White House and the Capitol building, both skilled and unskilled, were actually black slaves? When the pay chits of these workers were found in the National Archives, it became a national story.

The shock was not that the slaves did some of the work but that it hadn't been widely known. Why had this fascinating story, that the symbols of our freedom were in part created by those denied freedom, not been told?

I could have told it. As an African American, a writer, and a historian, I knew more than most Americans about the contributions of my people. I had seen the pay records of African Americans, both slave and free, who had fought as soldiers in the Revolutionary War to help create this country in the first place. I have records of blacks who served on the early privateers fighting against the powerful British navy. I had read the newspaper accounts of Andrew Ellicott's coming to the Federal District and bringing Benjamin Banneker, a black mathematician, to aid him. Even earlier, I knew what the slaveholders knew, that the men and women being brought into this country as slaves brought skills with them. I had seen the advertisement stating that a boatload of Africans were experienced in grain culture and the runaway advertisement saying that an escaped African had been an iron worker in his own country.

James Hoban, the architect who held legal title to two of the workers, was from Charleston, South Carolina, where blacks had been building plantation homes and furniture for years, as well as much of the grillwork that graces the city even today.

But it's up to me, and other historians, to document the efforts of these workers and to tell their story. We need to tell the story of the land clearers and the builders. We need to tell the story of those who defended a country in which they weren't equals. We need to ensure that their labor is valued, their courage appreciated, and their ingenuity acknowledged.

I believe that these hundreds of black workers who weren't free, as well as those who were, understood what they were creating and took some pride in their work. It's only human to be proud of your work, and the black carpenters whose names were on the rolls—Peter, Ben, Tom, and Harry—were as human as the architect or as any president who would live in the structure they helped to create. Recognizing the black men who helped in the construction of the White House is an ongoing part of building America.

Thomas Jefferson
1743–1826

❧ *Milton Meltzer* ❧

IT IS OFTEN FORGOTTEN or ignored that slavery helped raise Jefferson to the presidency. In the close-fought presidential election of 1800, he triumphed over the incumbent, John Adams, only because of the Constitution's "three-fifths clause." Placed in the founding document at the insistence of slaveholders, it required that each slave be counted as three-fifths of a person for purposes of congressional apportionment. The slaves themselves could not vote. But a southerner who owned, say, a thousand slaves could cast his one vote and, counting three-fifths of his slaves, six hundred more. Those extra votes gave the South a third more representatives in Congress than if white men alone had voted. This, in turn, meant a third more electoral votes—enough for Jefferson to edge out Adams in the final count.

The impact of that difference upon American life and democracy was enormous. Congress passed gag laws that prevented even a discussion about the abolition of slavery. And that difference favored the nomination of candidates who supported slavery.

During Jefferson's long political career, slavery and his support of it played a powerful role in shaping American life. Like many other leaders of the Revolution, Jefferson was a slaveholder. Monticello—his home—was built by slave labor, attended by slave labor, and supported by slaves who raised the tobacco, cotton, rice, indigo, and sugar that enriched their masters.

Early on, in public as well as private statements, Jefferson claimed that blacks were "inferior to the rest of mankind." He was justifying slavery as the proper condition for all nonwhites. He also supported the Missouri Compromise of 1820, which permitted the unlimited expansion of slavery in the lands west of the Mississippi.

There was one thing above all that Thomas Jefferson wanted to be remembered for—that he wrote the Declaration of Independence in 1776. In the Declaration is the phrase "All men are created equal."

You wonder how deeply the men who wrote and signed that Declaration believed in equality. As its author, Jefferson made a magnificent contribution. But neither he nor the other Founding Fathers were demigods. They were intelligent, brave, resourceful, but like all mortals, limited by flaws of character and failures of imagination.

White House Colonial Kitchen Gardens

❖ ❖ ❖ ❖ ❖ ❖ ❖ ❖ ❖ ❖ ❖ ❖ ❖ ❖

STEPHANIE LOER

illustrated by S. D. SCHINDLER

THOMAS JEFFERSON WAS A MAN ahead of his time when it came to tomatoes. A great tomato debate had been stewing since the colonists first arrived. Until the mid-1800s, tomatoes were not widely accepted as a food in America. Some people considered them poisonous, because they are related to several poisonous plants. Jefferson, a lawyer, statesman, philosopher, scientist—and enthusiastic gardener—did much to settle the question. He grew tomatoes and ate tomatoes both raw and cooked.

No early American gardener wrote as extensively about his garden as did the country's third president. From his diaries we know that at his Virginia home, Monticello, his vegetable garden contained more than seventy different species of vegetables. Peas were his favorite.

When Jefferson moved to the White House, a kitchen garden already existed. Kitchen gardens, named because of their proximity to the kitchen door, supplied families with vegetables for the table and herbs for medicinal remedies. The first kitchen garden at the White House was planted at President John Adams's request. While inspecting the president's house during its construction, Adams expressed concern about the lack of a kitchen garden. One was immediately planted and harvested before the Adamses arrived, in November 1800.

It seems probable that during Jefferson's tenure and well into the nineteenth century, the White House vegetable garden that spread southwest from the West Wing supplied most of the needs of the table. It was tended by a "kitchen gardener," who was a member of the house- and groundskeeping staff.

The early White House gardens featured a variety of vegetables and herbs, including corn, beans, and pumpkins grown with a planting technique learned from American Indians. Other mainstays were root crops, cabbages, peas, squashes, onions, lettuce, cucumbers (sometimes called cowcumbers), and radishes. Herbs were used for medicinal purposes as well as for flavoring and fragrance. Chamomile, dill, and mint were used for digestive problems. Marigolds kept deer out of the garden, and tansy repelled insects. Parsley was a breath cleanser. Thyme was used as an antiseptic, and yarrow was an anti-inflammatory.

As time progressed, produce was bought directly from farms and markets, and the vegetable garden became less of a necessity to the White House kitchen. After 1844, there is no mention of a "kitchen gardener" in the housekeeping records.

JEFFERSON'S MONSTROUS BONES

Barbara Kerley

In the late eighteenth century, decades before the discovery of dinosaurs,
scientific men like Thomas Jefferson were fascinated by fossils.

WHEN THOMAS JEFFERSON RODE into Philadelphia in March 1797 to be sworn in as vice president, he hauled a strange load in his wagon.

Bones. Monstrous bones.

Leg bones, paw bones, even a claw seven inches long. The bones were fossilized, clearly very old. But what animal had they come from?

The bones had been discovered by workmen digging in a cave in Jefferson's native state of Virginia. Jefferson—known by many to have a keen interest in fossils—had been eager to examine them. Through careful study, he determined that they belonged to an animal never before described by scientists. He named this animal *Megalonyx*, "Great Claw."

Jefferson gave the bones to the American Philosophical Society in Philadelphia, and his description of them was one of the first papers written on vertebrate fossils by an American.

Jefferson was fascinated by Great Claw, but the fossils that most deeply captured his imagination were of a different animal, an animal so mysterious that for decades, scientists all over the world had simply called it American *incognitum*, "unknown."

Throughout the 1700s, fossilized remains of *incognitum* had been found in the Hudson River Valley in New York and at Big Bone Lick on the Ohio River. The first *incognitum* fossil—a huge tooth weighing almost five pounds—seemed to some scholars in 1705 to have come from a human giant.

Over the years, more *incognitum* fossils had been uncovered, including tusks. *Incognitum,* it turned out, was an elephantlike creature. Similar tusks and bones found in Siberia came from a beast the local tribesmen there called *mammut.* Soon, scientists like Jefferson began calling the American *incognitum* by a new name: mammoth.

Jefferson eagerly sought out all the information he could find about the mammoth. He studied fossils and read other scientists' thoughts on the tusks and the teeth, which scientists called "grinders." Was the mammoth a placid plant eater, with tusks pointing upward like an elephant, or a fierce meat eater, whose downward-pointing tusks could rip the flesh of its prey? Jefferson also debated the fate of the mammoth. He knew that, according to American Indian traditions, the mammoth still lived in the isolated wilderness of the North American continent. Like many scientists of the day, Jefferson also believed that no animal created by God could ever become extinct.

Each new mammoth discovery was exciting to Jefferson because it seemed to refute a theory from Europe that he found "very degrading to America." The celebrated French scientist Georges-Louis Leclerc De Buffon had suggested that, compared to animals found in Europe, American animals were smaller and weaker.

But Jefferson was proud of his country and its hard-won independence from England. He was sure America could grow animals just as well as any other country. The massive mammoth fossils—bigger than any fossils found in Europe at that time—seemed to prove Buffon wrong.

Jefferson was delighted when, in 1801, his friend Charles Willson Peale exhumed enough mammoth fossils from the Hudson River Valley to reconstruct an entire skeleton for his museum in Philadelphia. The towering skeleton stood eleven feet tall, with tusks ten feet long.

Jefferson, however, had grander plans: after he became president, he asked Meriwether

Lewis to explore the recently purchased Louisiana Territory, a vast tract of land west of the Mississippi River. Jefferson told him to make a careful record of the flora and fauna:

> . . . the soil and face of the country, its growth and vegetable productions . . . the animals of the country . . . the remains and accounts of any which be deemed rare or extinct . . .

In other words, Lewis should keep his eyes peeled for *live* Great Claws and mammoths.

Before meeting up with his co-captain for the expedition, William Clark, Lewis stopped by Big Bone Lick on the Ohio River to collect fossils for the president. Lewis wrote that he was sending Jefferson some "handsome specimens," including an immense mammoth tusk and a "grinder," its roots embedded in a lump of the Lick's clay. He boxed up the specimens to ship to Jefferson.

Unfortunately, the boat sank at Natchez, Mississippi. Disappointed, Jefferson waited to hear more news of Lewis, Clark, and their band of explorers.

The expedition made it all the way to the Pacific Ocean and back again. Along the way, Lewis recorded 178 plants and 122 animals new to science. But, Lewis regretfully informed the president when the expedition returned in 1806, he didn't find any Great Claws or mammoths.

Jefferson was discouraged, more so when a poem was published that mocked the expedition for all it *didn't* accomplish:

On the Discoveries of Captain Lewis

. . . starting from the Atlantick shore
By fair and easy motion
He journeyed *all the way by land*
Until he met the ocean. . . .

What marvels on the way he found
He'll tell you, if inclin'd, sir—

But *I* shall only now disclose
The things he *did not* find, sir.

He never with a mammoth met
However you may wonder;
Not even with a Mammoth's bone,
Above the ground or under. . . .

Still, Jefferson didn't give up his quest to learn all he could about the mysterious beasts. Two months after the expedition's return, Jefferson asked Clark, who was headed to St. Louis, to stop by Big Bone Lick on his way. For several weeks, Clark and ten workers dug up bones: jawbones, leg bones, skulls, ribs, grinders, and—most important—tusks. Clark had found mammoths.

Clark boxed up the bones and shipped them to Jefferson. When the boxes arrived several months later, the delighted president spread the bones out on the floor of the unfinished East Room in the White House. He gave most of them to the American Philosophical Society in Philadelphia and the National Institute in France for further study. But he kept a few bones—jaws with the grinders still attached—for himself.

Soon after, Jefferson learned that the American *incognitum* was not a mammoth after all. Scientists in France had determined it was an entirely different animal, "which they have given the name of mastodon," Jefferson wrote to Clark, "from the protuberance of its teeth." But while more and more scientists accepted the concept of extinction, Jefferson still hoped that a live mastodon and Great Claw would one day be found.

In 1822, four years before his death, scientists honored Jefferson for the pioneering work he'd done on Great Claw: they officially named the species *Megalonyx jeffersonii*. It was a fitting tribute to this extraordinary man who spent much of his adult life studying bones.

BONES ON THE FLOOR
ILLUSTRATION BY
BRIAN SELZNICK

An Unusual Guest

Elizabeth Cody Kimmel

IN 1805, THE WHITE HOUSE played host to a peculiar four-legged guest, the likes of which no Washingtonian had ever laid eyes upon before. The little animal was one of the smaller discoveries made by President Jefferson's Corps of Discovery, a group of men sent to explore the unknown wilderness of the newly purchased Louisiana Territory and beyond, crossing unmapped lands to the very edge of the continent. Heading the endeavor were Meriwether Lewis and William Clark, co-commanders of the Corps.

This cross-country expedition of Lewis and Clark and their Corps of Discovery had been years in the making. Thomas Jefferson had long dreamed of what lay west of the Mississippi River in territory few citizens had even glimpsed. In 1803 he brought his dream into reality by organizing an expedition that would ascend the Missouri River to its source and continue west to the Pacific Ocean. Jefferson charged the Corps with establishing friendly relations with American Indian tribes, expanding trading possibilities, mapping the new territory, and seeking a Northwest Passage water route to the Pacific. Of equal importance, Lewis and Clark were instructed to discover and catalog new species of plants and animals and to collect information about the ways and customs of the American Indian tribes they encountered. With the recent acquisition of the enormous Louisiana Territory, approximately 800,000 miles of land west of the Mississippi, the need for accurate maps and detailed information about those lands had never been more pressing.

The Corps of Discovery departed St. Charles, Missouri, in May of 1804 and was comprised of forty men, three boats, and one Newfoundland dog named Seaman. By mid-September the expedition was making its way upriver through the Great Plains of present-day Nebraska and South Dakota, spending one day struggling to catch the president an oddly charming animal Lewis referred to as a barking squirrel. When the Corps finally established their winter camp near a Mandan village in what would become North Dakota, they had already visited with the Yankton and Teton Sioux and the Arikara tribe, and were now becoming friendly with both the Mandan and Hidatsa people. Among the Hidatsa was a young Shoshone woman named Sacagawea, who would eventually play a significant role in the expedition. The Corps had collected scores of plant and animal specimens, along with a wealth of geographical information about the territory through which they had traveled. During the winter months at camp, Lewis and Clark worked tirelessly to organize reports, sketches, and maps to send to President Jefferson, along with pressed plants and flowers and the bones and hides of newly discovered species such as the jackrabbit, the antelope, and the coyote. The barking squirrel, now known as a prairie dog, remained alive and well and was sent along with the shipment in a little crate.

When spring came, the Corps of Discovery continued through the upper Missouri into territory then completely unknown to any citizen of the United States. America's first scientific expedition was now truly seeing what no American had seen before. In Montana they battled grizzly bears and the Great Falls of the Missouri River. With the help of their Indian companion, Sacagawea, they established contact with the Shoshone Indians, who traded them horses and provided information for the route across the massive Rocky Mountains. After barely surviving the crossing, they recovered with the Nez Perce tribe before continuing on to the Clearwater River. From the Clearwater to the Snake and ultimately the Columbia River, the Corps of Discovery crossed through what are now Washington State and Oregon. By November of 1805, the Corps had reached the Pacific Ocean. They could go no farther. The expedition established a winter camp, Fort Clatsop, and settled in.

At the President's House in Washington, Jefferson had no direct word from Lewis and Clark but received a shipment from them in August of 1805. The reams of information and sketches and the crates of American Indian materials such as a luxurious buffalo robe gave a tantalizing glimpse of what the Corps had seen and what they might yet see. Among the items was the prairie dog that the Corps had taken such great pains to capture—the animal was healthy and none the worse for its journey. Jefferson was vacationing at his Monticello home when the shipment arrived, and he sent orders that the prairie dog be cared for carefully until his return to Washington in early October. Thus the future White House housed one of its most unusual and distinguished visitors—a furry ambassador from the Great Plains and a symbol of all that had yet to be learned about the newest territory of the United States.

Lewis and Clark and their Corps of Discovery returned to civilization in September of 1806, two years and four months after their departure. Only one of their men had died—from an attack of appendicitis. Because of the Corp's accomplishments and Lewis and Clark's meticulous collection and recordation of scientific information, Americans received a storehouse of knowledge about the life and nature of an enormous portion of their young country.

And, however briefly, a prairie dog was President Jefferson's guest at the White House.

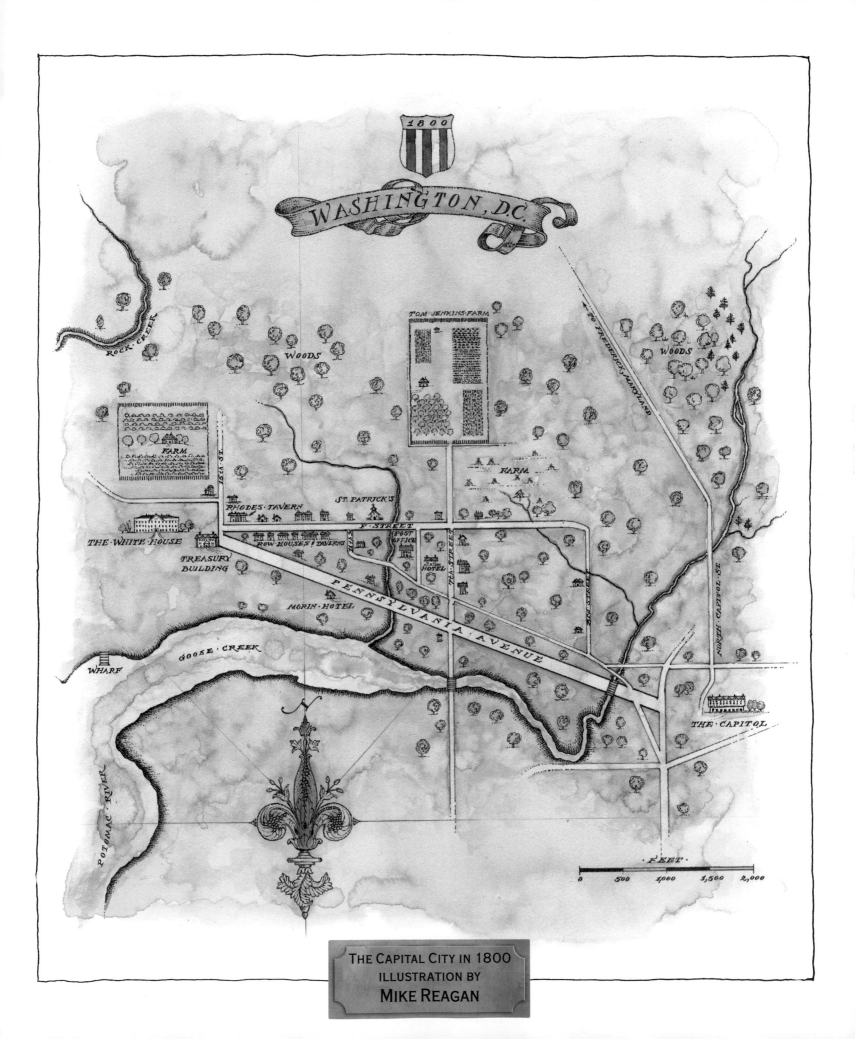

THE CAPITAL CITY IN 1800
ILLUSTRATION BY
MIKE REAGAN

PART II

STRUGGLING TO STAND

ILLUSTRATION BY
WENDELL MINOR

THE WHITE HOUSE PREPARES FOR WAR: 1812

⠶⠶⠶

RALPH KETCHAM

THOUGH THE UNITED STATES HAD WON its independence fair and square, it continued to have difficulties with Great Britain in the years following the American Revolution. The British remained in American territory along the Great Lakes and provided support to the Indians on America's frontiers. Then, as war raged between Great Britain and France during the early 1800s, Britain attempted to impede American trade with France through a variety of assaults on U.S. ships—"impressment," or the capture of American sailors off American vessels into the harsh discipline of the Royal Navy, being the chief and most humiliating of these actions. Convinced that the young nation could no longer yield to such outrageous practices, President James Madison asked Congress in 1812 to prepare for yet another war with Britain.

Madison had long been committed to diplomacy and commercial restrictions as ways to avoid war. Among other things, he feared the harmful effects of wartime measures— such as conscription, war spending, laws restricting civilian movement, restraints on freedom of expression, and interference with political processes—on American self-government. However, a "long Train of Abuses" could justify measures of force, as they had in 1776. After a decade of largely failed peaceful efforts to sustain neutral rights on the high seas, the time had come for action, and Madison was ready to fight.

The winter of 1811 to 1812 started badly. A "bilious fever" caused by the unfinished, never-successful Chesapeake and Ohio Canal filled the halls of Congress in December with the "dread of contagion." As Congress gathered, Dolley Madison prepared for a busy social season of receptions, parties, and dances at the White House (at this time usually referred to as the "President's House"). Also living at the White House most of the time before its destruction by British forces in August 1814 were Dolley's sister Anna Cutts (with her soon-to-be five children) and widowed sister, Lucy Washington (with her three young boys)—both beautiful and admired belles, centers of attention at all social events. Two of President Madison's nephews, Alfred and Robert Madison, his stepson, Payne Todd, and his private secretary, Edward Coles (also Dolley's cousin), also resided at the White House during the social season. All were eligible young males who entertained both daughters of congressmen and a string of other young women, relatives, and friends. Prominent among the young ladies was the most famous beauty of the era, Betsy Patterson of Baltimore, who had captivated, married, and then been abandoned by Napoleon's brother Jérôme. Thus, even though the Madisons were themselves childless, the White House vibrated with busy children, glamorous women, and constant parties and celebrations. The president reported that these made "sad inroads on his time," but he stuck to his routine, sleeping "very little, going to bed late and getting up frequently during the night to write or read; for which purpose a candle was always burning in the chamber." On occasion he came to the celebratory dinners, at which he usually took, a Pennsylvania congressman noted, "a liberal portion of wine, [and] became free and even facetious, telling with great archness many anecdotes."

Nonetheless, the president worked hard to persuade Congress to recruit, organize, and equip army and naval forces for the war he was sure was coming, to appoint civilian and military leaders, to prepare public opinion for the hostilities, and to exhaust every last diplomatic possibility, however unlikely, that might preserve peace. Noting Madison's difficulties, ex-President Jefferson, from Monticello, speculated that the notion that Congress, "a body containing 100 lawyers in it, should direct the measures of a war, is I fear, impossible." Strong earthquake shocks felt along the eastern seaboard in February 1812 were cited by antiwar New England clergymen as evidence of God's anger with

Madison and other bloodthirsty leaders—mostly Virginians, they noted. The British press, filled with anxiety at Napoleon's power as he prepared to capture Moscow and conquer Russia, condemned the United States for even supposing it could successfully fight Britain and for wasting time "TREMBLING and HESITATING on the slippery verge of war; . . . [which] tends to palsy the spirit, and to destroy the confidence of a nation." At a "family dinner" at the White House on a cold February evening, Richard Rush, son of Madison's old friend and colleague Dr. Benjamin Rush and newly part of the administration, nonetheless reported that the president, "*little* as he is in bulk, is, unquestionably above [the cabinet and Congress] in spirit and tone. While they are mere mutes, . . . he on every occasion, and to every body, talks freely . . . [and] says the time is ripe, and the nation, too, for resistance." Madison conferred with the British and French ministers, urged on members of Congress, and held off final action until a fast dispatch vessel, the *Hornet*, sent out in November 1811, finally returned. It arrived in New York on May 19, 1812, without news of British (or French) concessions. (It then took three days for the news to reach Washington, and two more to decode it.) Madison prepared his war message to Congress. Dolley Madison, worn out from receptions and celebrations attendant on the March 29 wedding in the White House of her sister Lucy to Supreme Court Justice Thomas Todd, reported that her "dear husband is overpowered with business" and that she was "the very shadow" of her husband.

On June 1, for more than half an hour, a clerk droned out Madison's call for war to a closed session of Congress. Madison put forth a straightforward list of grievances against Britain: impressment, attacks on American commerce within sight of its own harbors, "pretended blockades" that violated international law, and unjust "Orders in Council" that sustained "the monopoly which she covets for her own commerce and navigation." Though Madison left the "solemn question" of war or peace to Congress, as the Constitution required, he urged a declaration of hostilities and measures to support it.

Speaker Henry Clay pushed a war resolution through the House on June 4, but the Senate delayed for two weeks. Madison fretted anxiously. He appeared "very pale and extremely agitated" in his last conference with the British minister. To a New Yorker at a White House reception, Madison's look seemed "devoid of penetration; his face [was] crooked and wrinkled, . . . a little, old, dried-up politician." Madison's supporters feared that the British minister "dropped . . . bills of exchange . . . in the Senate" to secure antiwar votes. The minister even assigned an aide to keep pro-war Virginia senator Richard Brent too drunk to vote. The stalling tactics were finally overcome, though, and on June 17 the Senate voted 19 to 13 to declare war.

When Madison signed the declaration the next day, he exhorted "all good people of the United States, as they love their country . . . [to] exert themselves in preserving order, in promoting concord . . . and in . . . invigorating all the measures . . . for obtaining a speedy, a just, and an honorable peace."

In his first annual message to Congress during the war, written in the White House with the aid of his most trusted colleagues, James Monroe, Albert Gallatin, and Richard Rush, Madison explained the war's basic cause and objective: "The war . . . is a war neither of ambition nor of vainglory. . . . It is waged not in violation of the rights of others, but in maintenance of our own. . . . To have shrunk [from it] . . . would have struck us from the high rank where the virtuous struggles of our fathers had placed us, and have betrayed the magnificent legacy which we hold in trust for future generations. It would have acknowl-edged that on [water] . . . where all independent nations have equal and common rights, the American people were not an independent people, but colonists and vassals." Though the war led to the burning of the President's House by British grenadiers nearly two years later, the house's rebuilding during the last years of his administration confirmed Madison's view that the "Second War of American Independence" had been well worth the struggle.

The Burning of the White House

Susan Cooper

Let us suppose that this is from a letter sent in August 1814 by Ensign Thomas Burnham,
of the 85th Foot Regiment, to his parents in England:

INDEED I KNOW NOT WHY they continue this war, since their intent in 1812 was to throw us out of Canada and they have failed in that. But now we have avenged their burning of our Canadian capital, for we burned this week the house of their foolish President Madison who signed the war into being. You should have seen the flames!

All in one day we put them to flight at Bladensburg, and marched on Washington—often past swamps, which in this height of summer are very smelly. We were hot and dirty and tired but we marched very fine and orderly, with the American ragtag still scurrying away all around. You would have been proud, Father.

It was past sunset but the sky was red over the city, the Americans having set fire to their own Navy Yard to keep us from having the ships. Half our men marched to the seat of government, the Capitol, which we had orders to burn. General Ross was very firm against any looting, he said our task was only to destroy public buildings. He set a whole company to guard private houses along the main street, Pennsylvania Avenue, and shouted reassurances to the people still in their homes. Two of our men caught stealing were given a hundred lashes each. A third rogue was shot.

We marched up that great wide street in two columns, with two men in each column carrying a dark lanthorn. General Ross and Admiral Cockburn rode at our head. The President's House was a handsome broad building with stone walls and splendidly furnished rooms. The people had run away so fast that a banquet table was still heaped with food and drink for forty or more. We were all half-dead from hunger and thirst, and it was like heaven when General Ross cried, "Very well, lads—fall to!" The president's dinner disappeared in a wink, and we drank a toast in Madeira and water to "Peace with America and down with Madison!"

Then we piled furniture in the middle of this room and the drawing-room, sofas and tables and chairs, curtains and draperies, and set light to them. They flared up so fierce we had to scramble to get out. I heard strings twang as a piano blazed up. We stood watching outside. The flames burst out of the windows, shooting higher than the roof, and their noise was like thunder, a great continuous crackling roar.

Then on we marched, up towards the burning Capitol, the sky so bright with fire that you could have read a book by it. There were other public buildings we had to burn the next day. On our way, an American shouted to Admiral Cockburn, "If General Washington had been alive, you would not have gotten into this city so easily!"

"No, sir!" the Admiral shouted back. "If General Washington had been president, we should never have thought of coming here!"

And that was true, was it not?

Dolley Madison
RESCUES
GEORGE WASHINGTON

written and illustrated by DON BROWN

A GLAMOROUS WOMAN PERCHES high in her mansion, her spyglass sweeping the horizon for signs of her beloved husband gone to war. But she discovers only approaching disaster in the form of armed and angry men.

It's a scene you might expect a novelist to describe for a romantic thriller or a movie director to invent for a summer blockbuster. The tableau is altogether more gripping when you learn that it wasn't fabricated, that the woman was First Lady Dolley Madison, and that the mansion was the White House in 1814.

It is the second year of the War of 1812, between the United States and the British. The enemy is at the gates of the capital, and Dolley tries to spy her husband, President James Madison, rallying the soldiers. Instead, she sees "groups of [American] military, wandering in all directions, as if there was a lack of arms, or of spirit to fight for their own fireside." The English advance on the city, and panicked Washingtonians flee, including the militia assigned to protect the president's home. Deserted by nearly everyone, Dolley probably knows that she should run away, too.

And who would expect otherwise from her? She is the grande dame of Washington society, more familiar with the whistle of flutes than the whistle of bullets. Dolley's

celebrity rests on her skill for hosting not-to-be-missed parties while costumed in stunning gowns and striking turbans. She has "a smile and a pleasant word for everybody," and her grace has won over many of the bright lights of the young republic, including Thomas Jefferson, James Monroe, and Aaron Burr.

Dolley doesn't hesitate to show her grit. She has promised the president to protect important government documents housed in the president's mansion and is determined not to abandon them to the British. To the boom of nearby cannons, she packs the papers into the only carriage she can find. She is about to race away to safety when she remembers a portrait of George Washington.

She later wrote: "I insist[ed] on waiting until the large picture of General Washington [was] secured, and it require[d] to be unscrewed from the wall. The process was found too tedious for these perilous moments; I . . . ordered the frame to be broken, and the canvas taken out . . . and the precious portrait placed . . . in safe keeping."

Only then, after fulfilling her duty to her country, does Dolley Madison make good her escape, proving her own mettle and reminding us that history is wonderful for confounding our notions of the plausible and the improbable.

THE FIRST
WHITE HOUSE MEMOIR: 1865

Paul Jennings

ILLUSTRATED BY *R. Gregory Christie*

The following is an excerpt from the 1865 memoir of Paul Jennings, a former slave, along with the original editor's preface that accompanied it upon publication.

PREFACE: Among the laborers at the Department of the Interior is an intelligent colored man, Paul Jennings, who was born a slave on President Madison's estate in Montpelier, Va., in 1799. Paul was a "body servant" of Mr. Madison, till his death, and afterwards of Daniel Webster, having purchased his freedom of Mrs. Madison. His character for sobriety, truth, and fidelity, is unquestioned; and as he was a daily witness of interesting events, I have thought his recollections were worth writing down in almost his own language.

MR. MADISON, I think, was one of the best men that ever lived. I never saw him in a passion, and never knew him to strike a slave, although he had over one hundred; neither would he allow an overseer to do it. Whenever any slaves were reported to him as stealing or "cutting up" badly, he would send for them and admonish them privately, and never mortify them by doing it before others. They generally served him very faithfully. . . .

When Mr. Madison was chosen President, we came on and moved into the White House; the East Room was not finished, and Pennsylvania Avenue was not paved, but was always in an awful condition from either mud or dust. The city was a dreary place. . . .

Before the War of 1812 was declared, there were frequent consultations at the White House as to the expediency of doing it. Colonel Monroe was always fierce for it, so were Messrs. Lowndes, Giles, Poydrass, and Pope—all Southerners; all his Secretaries were likewise in favor of it.

Soon after war was declared, Mr. Madison made his regular summer visit to his farm in Virginia. We had not been there long before an express reached us one evening, informing Mr. M. of Gen. Hull's surrender. He was astounded at the news, and started back to Washington the next morning.

After the war had been going on for a couple of years, the people of Washington began to be alarmed for the safety of the city, as the British held Chesapeake Bay with a powerful fleet and army. Every thing seemed to be left to General Armstrong, then Secretary of War, who ridiculed the idea that there was any danger. But, in August, 1814, the enemy had got so near, there could be no doubt of their intentions. Great alarm existed, and some feeble preparations for defence were made. Com. Barney's flotilla was stripped of men, who were placed in battery, at Bladensburg, where they fought splendidly. A large part of his men were tall, strapping Negroes, mixed with white sailors and marines. Mr. Madison reviewed them just before the fight, and asked Com. Barney if his "Negroes would not run on the approach of the British?" "No sir," said Barney, "they don't know how to run; they will die by their guns first." They fought till a large part of them were killed or wounded; and Barney himself wounded and taken prisoner. One or two of these Negroes are still living here.

Well, on the 24th of August, sure enough, the British reached Bladensburg, and the fight began between 11 and 12. Even that very morning General Armstrong assured Mrs. Madison there was no danger. The President . . . rode out on horseback to Bladensburg to see how things looked. Mrs. Madison ordered dinner to be ready at 3, as usual; I set the table myself, and brought up the ale, cider, and wine and placed them in the coolers, as all the Cabinet and several military gentlemen and strangers were expected. While waiting, at just about 3, as Sukey, the house-servant, was lolling out of a chamber window, James Smith, a free colored man who had accompanied Mr. Madison to Bladensburg, galloped up to the house, waving his hat, and cried out, "Clear out, clear out!

General Armstrong has ordered a retreat!" All then was confusion. Mrs. Madison ordered her carriage, and passing through the dining-room, caught up what silver she could crowd into her old-fashioned reticule, and then jumped into the chariot with her servant girl Sukey, and Daniel Carroll, who took charge of them; Jo. Bolin drove them over to Georgetown Heights; the British were expected in a few minutes. Mr. Cutts, her brother-in-law, sent me to a stable on 14th street, for his carriage. People were running in every direction. . . .

I will here mention that although the British were expected every minute, they did not arrive for some hours; in the mean time, a rabble, taking advantage of the confusion, ran all over the White House, and stole lots of silver and whatever they could lay their hands on.

John Freeman (the colored butler) drove off in the coachee with his wife, child, and servant; also a feather bed lashed on behind the coachee, which was all the furniture saved, except part of the silver and the portrait of Washington (of which I will tell you by-and-by). . . .

It has often been stated in print, that when Mrs. Madison escaped from the White House, she cut out from the frame the large portrait of Washington (now in one of the parlors there), and carried it off. This is totally false. She had no time for doing it. It would have required a ladder to get it down. All she carried off was the silver in her reticule, as the British were thought to be but a few squares off, and were expected every moment. John Susè [Jean-Pierre Sioussat] (a Frenchman, then door-keeper, and still living) and Magraw, the President's gardener, took it down and sent it off on a wagon, with some large silver urns and such other valuables as could be hastily got hold of. When the British did arrive, they ate up the very dinner, and drank the wines, &c., that I had prepared for the President's party.

Another All-American Girl

★ ——————————— ★

short story by **MEG CABOT**

IT'S HAD QUITE A HISTORY. The White House, I mean.

And I should know. I'm there practically every day, on account of having once saved the president from being assassinated and his appointing me teen ambassador to the United Nations.

Oh, and the fact that I'm dating his son, David.

You might even have heard of me . . . Samantha Madison, eleventh grader, national heroine? Not that it's a big deal or anything. I don't actually even like talking about it.

Another thing I don't like talking about is this thing that happened one day when I accidentally-on-purpose fell asleep behind the national press secretary's desk. I mean, I was only resting my eyes for a second while the press secretary went down the hall to find some more Sharpies for me to sign headshots with.

But I guess I fell asleep, because the next thing I knew, I wasn't in the press secretary's office anymore. Instead I was standing outside the White House. Only it didn't look like the White House. At least the one I had come to know.

And not just because it was night. Not that you'd have known it, with half the summer sky lit orange from flames that seemed to be creeping ever closer. Washington, it appeared, was on fire.

But before I even had time to register any of that, this guy—who looked a lot like David, if David would ever have been caught dead in a tricorn hat—thrust all this stuff into my arms and went, "I think that's the last of it, Red."

Red? Who was he talking to? *Me?* I do have red hair, but David never calls me Red.

But then I heard someone calling the name *Brigitte*—somewhat urgently—and I turned around and found myself looking at a woman who seemed vaguely familiar.

Which was especially weird, since she was wearing a long, high-waisted gown, with her hair all piled up on top of her head. I don't know too many people who dress that way. OK, any.

"Don't just stand there gawking, Brigitte," the familiar-looking woman said to me. "Bring those here. Hurry, won't you? They'll be here within the hour." She flinched as an explosion ripped through the night sky. "Oh, dear," she said, looking off in the direction of a new burst of flame. "They've set fire to another munitions depot."

Totally shocked at how this woman could be so calm when things were *exploding* around us—not to mention the fact that she was calling me Brigitte—I surrendered the armful of parchment rolls I was holding.

I realized several things all at once at that moment. The first was that the lady was Dolley Madison, wife of James Madison, fourth president of the United States. I finally recognized her from the portrait hanging in the First Ladies' Gallery.

The second? James Madison was president during the War of 1812, which is when the British burned down Washington, in 1814. Including the White House. Which was what we were standing in front of.

The third was that somehow I had done one of those space-time-continuum time-travel thingies. Into someone else's body.

And the fourth was that I was in trouble. Big trouble.

"The British!" I screeched. I mean, we get along with the British *now* and all. But back then, those dudes totally wanted to off us. "They're coming! We've got to motor!" Then, seeing the confused expressions on the faces in front of me, I corrected myself. "I mean, flee! Flee!"

"That's what we're doing, Brigitte," Dolley Madison said calmly. "We're leaving now."

And then the cute guy in the hat was helping her into the seat of an extremely unreliable-looking buggy. It didn't look like the kind of carriage you'd expect to find the First Lady riding in.

"I know as personal maid to the First Lady, you're used to better, Red," Tricorn Hat said to me with a smirk, noticing my expression. "But this will have to do, as it was all I could find."

Personal maid to the First Lady? Was *that* who I was?

"Mrs. Madison." Tricorn had helped me climb onto the seat beside the driver. "Let me come with you. I've got a pistol—"

"Thomas," was Mrs. Madison's calm reply. "You're a brave boy—far braver than that regiment my husband left here to protect me, who fled at the first sign of the British forces. But someone must deliver this message to the president at Bladensburg"—she handed a folded-up piece of paper to Thomas—"so that he might know I'm safe . . . and, more importantly, so are his papers. Will you do that for me, Thomas?"

Thomas took the note and said, "If that's what you wish, Mrs. Madison." Then he looked at me and went, "Take care of her, Red," and winked.

I didn't know which to feel more insulted by—the wink or his utter lack of concern for what might happen to *me*.

And, OK, I realize I'm a twenty-first-century girl trapped in a nineteenth-century French maid's body, and I can take care of myself.

But still!

Before I had a chance to mention this, the driver flicked the reins and our carriage took off with a lurch. Soon we were careening down the streets of Washington—but not the Washington I'd grown up in. This looked more like a village.

Only this village was on fire. The driver turned our horse away from the flames and sent us clattering over dirt roads—empty, as everyone but Mrs. Madison had fled the besieged city days before—raising a cloud of dust that settled over our hair and clothes.

So maybe it wasn't any wonder that, when we finally halted in front of a small, peaceful farmhouse and the driver went to the door and asked if we could take shelter there for the night, the answer was a resounding no.

But when we were turned away from the next farmhouse and then the next, it soon became apparent that the problem wasn't our appearance at all. . . . It was who we were.

"President's wife, is it?" asked the last farmer. "Abandoned by her own husband, just like her husband abandoned Washington to the British! Well, this ought to give him a taste of his own medicine."

And the farmer slammed the door in the driver's face!

"No, Brigitte, no," Mrs. Madison said, seizing my arm as I attempted to clamber from the carriage to give that farmer a piece of my mind.

"But—" I sputtered. "How dare he? You're the First Lady!"

But Mrs. Madison said, "Brigitte, this is America, remember? People have the right here to express their own opinions."

But as we pulled up to yet another sleepy farmhouse, I knew what I had to do. I leaped from the buggy before either my mistress or the driver could stop me, strode up to the door, and pounded on it with all my might.

It was opened by a sleepy farmer who, along with his wife, stood rubbing his eyes and gazing at me in the light from the candle he held.

"Pray excuse me," I said. "But we come from Washington, which has fallen to the British and is burning even as we speak. May we please pass the night under your roof?"

The farmer's wife looked horrified.

"Washington, fallen to the British? Good heavens! Of course you must come in," she cried, and the First Lady made haste to do so. It wasn't until Mrs. Madison's face became visible in the light thrown by the farmer's candle that his wife gasped and said, "But you're . . . you're President Madison's wife!"

Mrs. Madison gave the farmer and his wife a tired smile. "I am," she said. "It's very kind of you to—"

"But you can't stay here!" The farmer's wife looked alarmed. "What if the British discover that we've sheltered you? They might set the crops afire!"

"What if they do?" I demanded. "It's a small price to pay for helping, in her time of need, one of the greatest First Ladies this country has ever known . . . one who risked her own life to save this!"

And I unrolled one of the things Mrs. Madison had made sure I'd stowed into the carriage . . . a portrait from the White House that the First Lady had cut from its frame at the last minute before we'd left Washington, to make sure it didn't fall into British hands.

Both the farmer and his wife gasped.

"That's George Washington!" the farmer cried. And his expression softened. "Well . . . I suppose letting you stay for one night won't hurt. . . ."

No sooner had we sat down than Mrs. Madison reached beneath the table and, laying a hand on mine, squeezed my fingers. When I glanced at her, she mouthed the words *Thank you,* looking immensely grateful.

That's when I woke up. Blinking, I found the White House press secretary staring down at me, holding a bunch of Sharpies and going, "Sam? Are you all right? Looks like you were having a bad dream."

Sitting up, I looked around. I was still in the White House, all right. Not the one I—I mean, Brigitte—had fled from, but the one that was built after the first one burned to the ground that horrible August night in 1814 . . . and from which Dolley Madison escaped in the nick of time, saving George Washington's famous portrait, which is in the National Gallery today.

That White House is gone forever. But the current one's been around for a while . . . and, with any luck, will *stay* around for a while more.

FROM the WALLS of the WHITE HOUSE

KATHLEEN KRULL

ILLUSTRATED BY ROBERT BYRD

THE WHITE HOUSE is a major American art museum. Its walls glow with some five hundred paintings full of history and fascinating people. Some of the figures are famous—like George Washington in all his glory—while others are less well-known.

Five portraits of American Indians hang in the White House, courtesy of President James Monroe. In 1821, he invited a group of American Indians to the White House to give them "peace medals." The Bureau of Indian Affairs, trying to show off the wealth of the United States, asked professional portrait painter Charles Bird King to paint the American Indians' portraits. The great chief Petalesharro, a Pawnee, wears several beaded necklaces and a lavish warbonnet made of eagle feathers. He also wears the large "peace medal"—with President Monroe's profile on it. It turned out that Monroe's ulterior motive was to remind the American Indians of America's authority over them. This meeting, as with so many others between chiefs and presidents, failed to result in establishing peace.

VISITING THE GREAT FATHER

JOSEPH BRUCHAC
ILLUSTRATED BY MAX GRAFE

AMERICAN INDIANS HAVE LONG SEEN the White House as their house, too. Black Hawk of the Mesquaki sat in Andrew Jackson's study, smoking the calumet of peace with Old Hickory. Red Cloud of the Lakotas and his wife accepted bouquets of summer flowers from President and Mrs. Grant at a gala reception.

From the time of Jefferson on, thousands of American Indian leaders were welcomed to the White House. Many were awed and impressed. When Hoowaneka, a Winnebago chief, met John Quincy Adams in 1828, "So large and beautiful was the President's House . . . that when I entered it, I thought I was in heaven."

Some Native guests were fluent in English, but not all presidents understood that. Lincoln's Secretary, John Hay, wrote an amused account of Lincoln receiving a mission-educated Potawatomi leader. "Where live now?" Lincoln said as he shook the man's hand. "When go back Iowa?" The Indian was shocked that the "White Father" spoke such poor English.

Many of these Native ambassadors were photographed at the White House. Images of presidents meeting Indians arrayed in buckskins and feathers were as familiar to newspaper readers of the time as Rose Garden conferences with foreign diplomats are to TV viewers today.

One of the most poignant photos of an Indian delegation comes from March 1863. Eight white men and women, including Mary Todd Lincoln, stand behind several Southern Cheyennes seated on the ground in the White House Conservatory. Within two years, all of the Indian leaders in the picture were dead. Yellow Wolf succumbed to pneumonia a few days after the photo was taken (neither the first nor the last Indian to die while in Washington, where cool weather brought pneumonia and summer's heat, malaria). Lean Bear was shot by Army troops mistaking him for a hostile. War Bonnet and Standing in the Water perished in the Sand Creek Massacre.

The American Indian who most often came to the White House during this period was Ely Parker of the Senecas. Repeatedly sent by his people to lobby against their removal from New York, he was entertained by presidents Polk, Taylor, Fillmore, Pierce, Buchanan, and Lincoln, then served as Grant's Commissioner of Indian Affairs. On New Year's Day 1847, Parker went to his first White House reception. It was so crowded that visitors had to leave by climbing out an open window. Traditionally attired, Parker caused a stir. As he wrote, "Close inspection and my native costume soon assured them that it was a savage brave, who thus had the audacity and impudence to mingle with the nobility." Parker's everyday dress was that of a middle-class white man, but like many Native visitors to the White House, he utilized the strategic advantage of looking like a "real Indian" to be welcomed in his Great Father's house.

Calling the president the "Great Father," as many nineteenth-century Indian leaders did, was also a considered choice. Visitors purposefully used this term to indicate that the chief executive should act like a proper Indian father, providing for and defending his Native children. Since that time, the term *Great White Father* has often appeared in print as the Indian name for the president. But in the language of treaties and Native oral traditions, he is and always has been the Great Father, without the racial separation introduced by the word *White*.

Sneaking Into
Adams Field

MICHAEL WINERIP

FOR A WHILE THERE, it looked like being born in Quincy, Massachusetts, was a sure ticket to the White House. Two of our first six presidents, John Adams and John Quincy Adams, were born in Quincy, but since then, as the city has filled up with people like me, there has been a 180-year drought. I must admit, I feel partly responsible for the dramatic drop-off. Growing up in Quincy, I constantly brushed up against history and yet absorbed none of it.

By the early 1960s, Quincy was no longer home to the Protestant landed gentry. It was a working-class, mainly Catholic shipyard town. Kids didn't have much money and played in the streets. I can remember when I was little, riding by the Adams birthplaces—two red, drab, totally undistinguished saltbox homes. And when I should have been thinking "What a great country we live in that these two men could go from such humble origins to becoming president," what I was actually thinking was "Wicked puny houses." The Adams Mansion, the family homestead, was more befitting a president, though what I remember most about it was cupboards filled with china, not my strong point as a boy or man.

Now, I do have strong, affectionate memories of Adams Field, the best baseball field in town, named in the presidents' honor (there's a bronze statue of the two of them out front) and so prized that it was locked when not in use. To me and my twelve-year-old friends, that lovely baseball field was actually our own personal golf course. Summer mornings during my junior-high years, we'd sneak under the left-field fence at Adams. Between the seven of us, we owned two golf clubs—a 3-iron and a putter. Our golf balls came from the woods by the Wollaston Golf Club, and we shared a single tee. We'd dig three holes in the Adams outfield—in left, center, and right fields—then tee off from second base.

That life in Quincy could not have been more different from John Quincy Adams's upbringing. By age ten, young John Quincy was crossing the Atlantic to accompany his father on European diplomatic missions. During the voyage over, the boy, who was already bilingual, tutored two Frenchmen in English. By 1781, at fourteen (an age when I was running for ninth-grade vice president against Susan Brophy at Central Junior High), John Quincy was living on his own in Russia, serving as translator for the American diplomat Francis Dana at the Russian royal court.

When it came time for college, having been exposed to the great European universities, John Quincy had mixed feelings about attending "a small school like Harvard." He needed just a year to get his degree there, finishing second in a class of fifty-one. By age thirty-five, he was a U.S. senator; at forty-two, he was minister to Russia (and a close friend of Czar Alexander I). At fifty-eight, he became the sixth president.

And ever since, people from Quincy like me who wanted to go to the White House had to stand in line with all the other tourists. Still, there were a few things John Quincy Adams and we boys playing golf in the Adams outfield shared. We all had bossy, driven mothers who did their best to save us from eternal damnation. Even when John Quincy was a U.S. senator, his mother, Abigail, would send nasty notes nagging him about not shaving often enough, not dressing neatly enough, and eating poorly.

Like John Quincy before us, we loved to swim for free. In Quincy, you had two choices: Wollaston Beach, a calm, safe public beach; or the quarries—the old granite mines that had filled with crystal clear rainwater and were dangerous. Almost every summer some kid would die jumping off a high rock ledge into the quarries, but it never stopped us.

As president, John Quincy loved swimming in the Potomac—much to the horror of proper Washington—and once nearly drowned. On June 13, 1825, rumors of his drowning began circulating after the president was forced to jump from a sinking rowboat fully clothed, his waterlogged long-sleeved shirt and baggy pants nearly pulling him under. After struggling to the shore, he stripped while a servant searched for help. I like to think that that was the Quincy in John Quincy Adams.

The truth is, I think John Quincy would have been miserable in the working-class Quincy I grew up in. We Adams Field golfers were classic hoi polloi, and John Quincy was no man of the masses. As he said himself in his twelve-volume diary, "I well know that I never was and never shall be what is commonly termed a popular man." Never a glad-hander, he was the last president you'd find on a coin or a bill. He was a man who believed electioneering was rude and disdained the easy publicity ops that today's politicians live off—he even turned down a chance to appear at ceremonies commemorating the fiftieth anniversary of the battle of Bunker Hill.

But there are many things that working-class kids of Quincy and beyond owe him. He was committed to publicly funded education and opportunity for all people. As president, he favored opening a public national university and a naval academy modeled on West Point. He wanted government-funded science research, including astronomy observatories. He supported federally funded roads, canals, bridges, and highways to encourage commerce and help the country grow. Most of these proposals, too far ahead of their time, were defeated during his presidency. But later in his life, he did become one of the nation's leading antislavery voices and defended the Africans from the slave ship *Amistad* who'd rebelled against the ship's crew. Serving as their lawyer, he helped them win their freedom before the Supreme Court.

Though John Quincy was a first-rate thinker, his lack of political skills doomed his administration to one term. But this, too, was admirable. At a time in the nineteenth century when most of the nations of the world were still picking their leaders based on bloodline, John Quincy Adams lived the democratic ideal. He was the son of a president who himself became president and understood that it was a position that had to be earned and could be lost. When he did lose after one term, he accepted it and was not too proud to take a few steps down the political ladder. He ran for a seat in the House of Representatives, where he served the final twenty years of his life.

John Quincy Adams may not have felt at home among the people, but he lived a life that served the people well. Some two hundred years after he was born, two of those idiotic Adams Field golfers, both graduates of the local Quincy public school, attended the same Harvard College that he and so many other presidents had. It was the early 1970s, a moment when our elite institutions were opening to working-class kids, women, Jews, blacks, Hispanics, Asians. If John Quincy Adams had been around to see it, I'm not sure he would have felt comfortable sitting on a bench in Harvard Yard, reminiscing about Quincy with my brother and me. But I feel certain that he would have defended our right to be there.

ANDY
AND
ME

short story by **Marguerite W. Davol**
illustrated by **Tom Pohrt**

I'LL BET A POSSUM'S TAIL you've heard of me—Davy Crockett, Coonskin Congressman from West Tennessee, a rip-roaring, alligator-wrestling, bear-hugging critter, all right, fresh from the frontier. You know, that feller down there in the White House—our seventh president, name of Andrew Jackson—can match me brag for brag.

Us cubs got born in log cabins to families scrabbling to feed us. As young whippersnappers, me and Andy didn't much cotton to school. You could fill an acorn cup with our book learnin' and have room left over. But nature learnin'? Well, wrestlin' with the wilderness—that was our schooling.

Like me, Andy was a feisty backwoodsman, fierce as a she-bear protecting her cubs. At thirteen, him and his brother joined the army but were captured by the British. When an officer ordered Andy to clean his boots, Andy wasn't about to stoop as low as a toad's toes, particularly for the enemy! Furious, the officer swung his sword. Andy still wears the scar on his forehead.

Orphaned at fourteen, Andy Jackson became wild as a willywaw, overindulging in horse races, cockfights, wrestling matches, and quarrels. With a temper quicker'n forked

lightning, he'd druther challenge a man to a duel as look slantindicular at him. I've heard tell he still wears a duel's bullet near his heart.

Clever as a crow, Andy reckoned the frontier lacked lawyers. He studied law, then became a mighty fair judge, although he backed up his decisions with a pair of pistols. When he was appointed Major General Jackson, I joined up, proud as a ring-tailed raccoon to fight with Andy's army. Slogging through alligator-rich swamps, battling mammoth mosquitoes peskier than the enemy, we won our battles against the Indians, then the British. I hunted bears so our troops wouldn't starve. Awed by Jackson's endurance, his troops nicknamed him Old Hickory. Yep, Andy was as tough as hickory wood.

After the wars, Andy got elected senator from Tennessee. All dignified he was, charming Washington's highfalutin polite society and its not-so-polite politicians. Andy stood out in a crowd—tall and thin as a rifle. Ladies buzzed around him like flies to syrup, despite his battle-scarred face.

Now, Congress thrives on honey-tongued oratory. Andy Jackson sure wouldn't win a spelling bee, but speechifying? That man could talk the bark off a tree and stack it for kindling. Once he pinned you with his steely-blue eyes, you were stuck worse'n a mule in mud.

I joined Congress, too, informing a Washington hotel clerk I was "Davy Crockett, half horse, half alligator, a . . . snapping turtle; can wade the Mississippi, leap the Ohio, ride upon a streak of lightning . . . whip my weight in wildcats, hug a bear too close for comfort, and eat any man opposed to Jackson."

Yep, us rugged frontier critters joined powerful politicians to push Andy for president. The 1828 campaign wasn't prettified, no sirree, with enough dirt-slinging to bury Florida. But Andrew Jackson won, the first president chosen by the people instead of shoveled in by Congress.

At Jackson's inauguration, the crowd went wild. Afterward, backwoodsmen, patricians, veterans all swarmed to his White House reception. Punch spilled; glassware and furniture got broken. Patent-leather pumps, alongside muddy boots, trampled the rugs. It was a right-smart rollickin' ruckus!

Imagine! My old friend Andrew Jackson, president of the United States! Mostly a powerful-good president, but we parted company when he hornswoggled the Indians into abandoning their homes and heading west. T'warn't my vote that put him into the White House a second term. Still, I'm proud to know Old Hickory, president of us common men.

THE WHITE HOUSE COW

RICHARD PECK

ILLUSTRATED BY BARRY ROOT

IN THE BESIEGED TWENTY-FIRST CENTURY, every public building is an armed camp, and every invited White House guest needs a security clearance. But it wasn't always so. The White House rose as the city of Washington was still carving itself out of swamp and slough. It stood without a fence in a town more blueprint than brick.

Even in the 1840s, the White House stood open to its neighborhood, according to one of the few anecdotes from the William Henry Harrison administration. Harrison lore is scant, because the old soldier (he was sixty-eight) lived only a month and a day of his presidency. His most famous role was as principal figure in the first White House funeral, lying in magnificent state in the East Room.

Still, a story of the living man survives. As a soldier, Harrison knew the value of victualing and noted the absence of a good milk cow on the premises. He went off on foot one market day and found a promising cow. But when the farmer heard where it was to be delivered, he thought he smelled a rat. Still, the buyer led the seller and the seller led the cow back to the White House. The president asked the farmer inside and even invited him to stay to breakfast.

By now the farmer, gravely skeptical, asked who his host might be, wondering if he wasn't being a little too free in his use of a house set aside for "old Granny Harrison."

"The people call me William Henry Harrison and have made me the president of the United States," the president is said to have replied with quiet dignity.

"Lord a'mighty!" the terrorized farmer yelled, plunging out of the room and the house and making tracks across the still-open country past any number of security checkpoints yet unbuilt.

ILLUSTRATION BY
TIMOTHY BASIL ERING

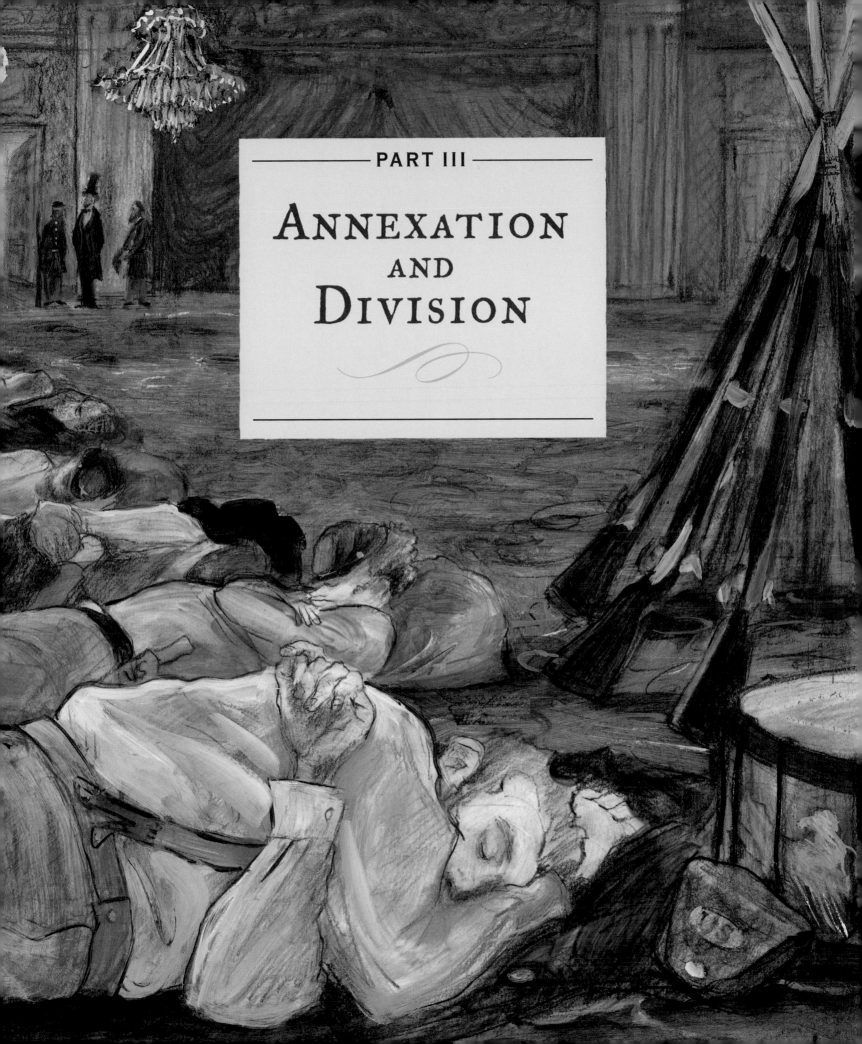

PART III

ANNEXATION AND DIVISION

From *American Notes*

CHARLES DICKENS
1842

illustrated by Claire Nivola

THE PRESIDENT'S MANSION is more like an English club-house, both within and without, than any other kind of establishment with which I can compare it. The ornamental ground about it has been laid out in garden walks; they are pretty, and agreeable to the eye; though they have that uncomfortable air of having been made yesterday, which is far from favourable to the display of such beauties.

My first visit to this house was on the morning after my arrival, when I was carried thither by an official gentleman, who was so kind as to charge himself with my presentation to the President.

We entered a large hall, and having twice or thrice rung a bell which nobody answered, walked without further ceremony through the rooms on the ground floor, as divers other gentlemen (mostly with their hats on, and their hands in their pockets) were doing very leisurely. Some of these had ladies with them, to whom they were showing the premises; others were lounging on the chairs and sofas; others, in a perfect state of exhaustion from listlessness, were yawning drearily. The greater portion of this assemblage were rather asserting their supremacy than doing anything else, as they had no particular business there, that anybody knew of. A few were closely eyeing the movables, as if to make quite

sure that the President (who was far from popular) had not made away with any of the furniture, or sold the fixtures for his private benefit.

After glancing at these loungers; who were scattered over a pretty drawing-room, opening upon a terrace which commanded a beautiful prospect of the river and the adjacent country; and who were sauntering, too, about a larger state-room called the Eastern Drawing-room; we went up-stairs into another chamber, where were certain visitors, waiting for audiences. At sight of my conductor, a black in plain clothes and yellow slippers who was gliding noiselessly about, and whispering messages in the ears of the more impatient, made a sign of recognition, and glided off to announce him. . . .

There were some fifteen or twenty persons in the room. One, a tall, wiry, muscular old man, from the west; sunburnt and swarthy; with a brown white hat on his knees, and a giant umbrella resting between his legs; who sat bolt upright in his chair, frowning steadily at the carpet, and twitching the hard lines about his mouth, as if he had made up his mind 'to fix' the President on what he had to say, and wouldn't bate him a grain. Another, a Kentucky farmer, six-feet-six in height, with his hat on, and his hands under his coat-tails, who leaned against the wall and kicked the floor with his heel, as though he had Time's head under his shoe, and were literally 'killing' him. A third, an oval-faced, bilious-looking man, with sleek black hair cropped close, and whiskers and beard shaved down to blue dots, who sucked the head of a thick stick, and from time to time took it out of his mouth, to see how it was getting on. A fourth did nothing but whistle. A fifth did nothing but spit. And indeed all these gentlemen were so very persevering and energetic in this latter particular, and bestowed their favours so abundantly upon the carpet, that I take it for granted the Presidential housemaids have high wages, or, to speak more genteelly, an ample amount of 'compensation:' which is the American word for salary in the case of all public servants.

We had not waited in this room many minutes, before the black messenger returned, and conducted us into another of smaller dimensions, where, at a business-like table covered with papers, sat the President himself. He looked somewhat worn and anxious, and well he might; being at war with everybody—but the expression of his face was mild and pleasant, and his manner was remarkably unaffected, gentlemanly, and agreeable. I thought that in his whole carriage and demeanour, he became his station singularly well. . . .

. . . I only returned to this house once. It was on the occasion of one of those general assemblies which are held on certain nights, between the hours of nine and twelve o'clock, and are called, rather oddly, Levees.

I went, with my wife, at about ten. There was a pretty dense crowd of carriages and people in the court-yard, and so far as I could make out, there were no very clear regulations for the taking up or setting down of company. There were certainly no policemen to soothe startled horses, either by sawing at their bridles or flourishing truncheons in their eyes; and I am ready to make oath that no inoffensive persons were knocked violently on the head, or poked acutely in their backs or stomachs; or brought to a standstill by any such gentle means, and then taken into custody for not moving on. But there was no confusion or disorder. Our carriage reached the porch in its turn, without any blustering, swearing, shouting, backing, or other disturbance: and we dismounted with as much ease and comfort as though we had been escorted by the whole Metropolitan Force from A to Z inclusive.

The suite of rooms on the ground-floor were lighted up, and a military band was playing in the hall. In the smaller drawing-room, the centre of a circle of company, were the President and his daughter-in-law, who acted as the lady of the mansion; and a very interesting, graceful, and accomplished lady too. One gentleman who stood among this group, appeared to take upon himself the functions of a master of the ceremonies. I saw no other officers or attendants, and none were needed.

The great drawing-room, which I have already mentioned, and the other chambers on the ground-floor, were crowded to excess. The company was not, in our sense of the term, select, for it comprehended persons of very many grades and classes; nor was there any great display of costly attire: indeed, some of the costumes may have been, for aught I know, grotesque enough. But the decorum and propriety of behaviour which prevailed, were unbroken by any rude or disagreeable incident; and every man, even among the miscellaneous crowd in the hall who were admitted without any orders or tickets to look on, appeared to feel that he was a part of the Institution, and was responsible for its preserving a becoming character, and appearing to the best advantage.

On Looking into
Dresses Worn by the "First Ladies"
of the White House (Paper Doll Cut-outs)
1938

NANCY WILLARD

illustrated with original book cover and paper dolls by
MAYBELLE MERCER

UNDER A PILE of books and clothes
in a thrift shop called Nearly New,
I found a book of paper dolls,
their clothes well drawn, topaz and blue,
crimson and pearl, the details fine,
the gowns arranged in headless rows
as if in a receiving line.

FRANCES CLEVELAND's gown was green,
stitched like a rose garden. The bolder
butterflies lit on the sheen
of Mrs. Cleveland's silken shoulder.

JANE PIERCE wore black with silver dots
and a black fringe on her lace shawl
in mourning for her son who died
two months before the inaugural ball.

IDA MCKINLEY's gown was cream
satin, with lace in front and back.
What I'll remember from that book
is not how fancy dresses look
but why Jane Pierce's dress was black.

Elizabeth Keckly

SEAMSTRESS TO FIRST LADY MARY TODD LINCOLN, 1861–1865*

story by
PATRICIA C. AND FREDRICK L. MCKISSACK

illustrated by
LEO AND DIANE DILLON

WHO ARE SOME OF YOUR OTHER CLIENTS?" Mrs. Lincoln asked the attractive African-American woman sitting across from her. The First Lady needed a seamstress to make a special dress for an affair the Tuesday following the inaugural. Mrs. Margaret McLean, the wife of Colonel Eugene McLean of Maryland, was one of Elizabeth Keckly's clients and a friend of Mary Lincoln's. Mrs. McLean had arranged for Mary to meet "Lizzie."

"I've made dresses for several ladies here in Washington," Lizzie answered. She named Mrs. McLean; Mary Ann Randolph Custis Lee, the wife of Colonel Robert E. Lee; Varina Davis, the wife of Senator Jefferson Davis; and several other prominent Washington wives. The First Lady knew or knew about some of these women, and she was impressed with the list. Lizzie knew Mary Lincoln would be. The First Lady had a sense of style and fashion, and choosing the "right" seamstress was as important as joining the proper social club.

Lizzie was also thinking about her future and what this commission might mean to her career. Since she had arrived in Washington, D.C., Lizzie's former contacts from St. Louis, Missouri, had helped her build a new clientele that had in a short time established her as the dressmaker for the capital's leading families. Now Lizzie was in the White House. It couldn't get any better, and it took all she had to contain her excitement. But she managed to sit calmly, a picture of composure, with her long, slender hands neatly folded in her lap.

"Who taught you how to sew?" the First Lady inquired.

"My mother, Agnes Hobbs, who was the plantation seamstress."

"Yes, I understand you were a slave at one time," said Mrs. Lincoln, frowning as if the unpleasant subject threatened to spoil the moment.

Lizzie was not embarrassed about having been a slave. She was proud to announce now that she was a free woman. "My son and I were freed when a number of my St. Louis clients bought our freedom. Four months ago, I moved here to Washington, D.C."

The First Lady asked a few more questions. Although Lizzie appeared poised and dignified, she was a bundle of nerves, but she answered each question thoughtfully and with confidence.

Suddenly, the First Lady blurted out in a rapid, high-pitched voice, "I warn you, I will not pay high prices just because I am the First Lady. If you are fair with me, you will have all the work you can possibly handle."

Lizzie remained very still and spoke in a quiet voice, the way she had when she was a small child on the plantation avoiding her mistress's unexpected anger. Lizzie was accustomed to clients who spoke to her gruffly, but without exception her clients had never questioned her integrity. If she hadn't needed the work so badly, she would have addressed the issue more directly. Instead she remained silent, eyes cast downward.

Slowly the First Lady seemed to relax. Inauguration nerves? Perhaps.

The two women negotiated and came to terms that were acceptable to both parties. Mrs. Lincoln commissioned a dress made of rose-colored moiré antique. The dress was to be completed by the end of the following week, which was an almost impossible job. But Lizzie was accustomed to completing impossible chores for an unappreciative master. She had come too far to miss this opportunity. Lizzie accepted Mary Lincoln's terms and promised to meet the deadline.

Lizzie knew that her career as a seamstress depended on the outcome of this very special dress for President Lincoln's wife. She put her heart and soul into every stitch.

Over the next few days, Lizzie worked night and day and even hired a lady to help in the cutting and pressing of the garment.

Tuesday evening was the night of the big affair. Lizzie finished putting the last stitches in the hem of the garment and hurried out to the carriage that was waiting to rush her to the White House. Lizzie was escorted upstairs, where Mrs. Lincoln was waiting impatiently.

Lizzie wondered why Mrs. Lincoln was so furious. What had she done? Lizzie had grown accustomed to the volatile mood swings of her former mistress, who could hug with one hand and slap with the other.

"You have failed me," Mrs. Lincoln wailed. "You are a total disappointment, and I am bitterly angry. You are late, and I cannot possibly be dressed in time."

But there was more than enough time. Lizzie decided that Mrs. Lincoln was probably suffering from a case of nerves and not really angry about anything Lizzie had or had not done. The experienced seamstress responded quietly, "Trust me, Mrs. Lincoln. We have time. I personally will dress you, and everything will be just fine."

The First Lady calmed down a bit as Lizzie arranged her hair and helped Mary Lincoln into the lovely dress, which fitted perfectly. Still, Mrs. Lincoln didn't totally relax until the door swung open and the president entered. He casually flopped on the sofa. "I declare, Mother, you look charming in that dress."

With that said, Mrs. Lincoln's smile brightened the room like a million candles glowing.

Later Elizabeth Keckly wrote in her autobiography, "I knew then that I would sew for Mrs. Lincoln again and again."

And she did. Throughout the Lincoln presidency, Lizzie was a frequent and welcome guest at the White House as personal seamstress to the First Lady. But more than that, Elizabeth Keckly became one of Mrs. Lincoln's closest friends, the first person she called for when President Lincoln was assassinated.

*Keckly is often spelled Keckley, because it was misspelled by the publisher of her autobiography. However, whenever Elizabeth wrote her name, she spelled it Keckly. Since she was a literate woman, we have chosen to spell her name the way she signed it.

High Spirits
in the
Lincoln White House

. . .

Russell Freedman

THE FIRST PRESIDENTIAL CHILDREN to live in the White House were the Lincolns' younger sons, eight-year-old Tad and eleven-year-old Willie. Their high-spirited antics amused their father, annoyed the household staff, and upset the formal decorum of the Executive Mansion.

The boys raced and shouted through the hallways, burst into their father's study in the midst of conferences, and played tricks on cabinet members. Tad would stand in front of the grand staircase and collect a nickel "entrance fee" from callers on their way to see the president. The youngsters collected a menagerie of pets—kittens, rabbits, a turkey, a pony they rode around the White House grounds, a goat that slept on Tad's bed, and a small dog named Jip that sat on the president's lap during meals and enjoyed the tidbits Lincoln slipped him.

Tad and Willie often played in the White House attic. One day they discovered the place near the roof where all the cords for the house's bell system came together; the cords ran down to various rooms where Lincoln or the staff could pull them when they wanted something. Tad started yanking all the cords at once, setting every bell in the house clanging and causing bedlam until the staff discovered what was going on.

Mary Lincoln had desks and a blackboard placed at one end of the state dining room and hired tutors for the boys. But Tad, wild and exuberant, had "no opinion of discipline," said Lincoln's secretary John Hay, and the tutors quickly became discouraged and quit, one after another. Unlike Tad, Willie was a fast learner. A gentle, warmhearted youngster, he liked to curl up with a book or jot down verse on a writing pad. He could call off the names of all the main railroad stations from New York to Chicago.

Lincoln adored his "two little codgers," bragging about them at every opportunity. He denied the boys nothing and seemed incapable of disciplining them. Relaxing with Willie and Tad, he found some relief from the terrible tensions and anxieties of the Civil War. He would join in their games, wrestle with them on the Oriental carpets, and read them stories with his spectacles on.

The boys were not unmindful of the war. They searched for rebels through an old telescope on the White House roof and staged military parades through the White House corridors, blowing horns and banging on drums. They had a soldier doll named Jack, dressed in the red and blue uniform of a French Zouave. It seems that Jack fell asleep while on guard duty; he was court-martialed and sentenced to death. Tad and Willie planned to bury him beneath a bush, but as they prepared the grave, the White House gardener suggested that perhaps the president might pardon him. Sure enough, a note on Executive Mansion stationery was presented to the boys: "The doll Jack is pardoned. By order of the President. A. Lincoln."

"Mr. Lincoln was very exceedingly indulgent to his children," Mary observed. "He always said, 'It is my pleasure that my children are free, happy, and unrestrained by parental tyranny. Love is the chain whereby to bind a child to its parents.'"

Mary Todd Lincoln Speaks of Her Son's Death, 1862

PAUL B. JANECZKO

When Willie died of the fever,
Abraham spoke the words
that I could not:
"My boy is gone.
He is actually gone."

Gone.
The word was a thunderclap,
deafening me to my wails
as I folded over his body,
already growing cold.

Gone.
The word was a curtain
coming down on eleven years,
hiding toy soldiers,
circus animals,
and his beloved train.

Gone.
The word was poison,
but poison that would not kill,
only gag me with its bitterness
as I choked on a prayer for my death.

Abraham spoke the words
that I could not:
"My boy is gone.
He is actually gone."
And I am left
with grief that
when spoken
shatters like my heart.

Memoir by Mary Henry

EYEWITNESS TO THE CIVIL WAR IN THE CITY OF WASHINGTON

SOUTHERN ARMY APPROACHING THE CITY OF WASHINGTON, July 1864

July 10th Sunday.

Several persons were called out of church this morning, exciting our curiosity, and on coming out after service we were startled by the intelligence that a large body of Southern troops 40 or 50,000 in number, were marching on Washington. They had thrown the city of Baltimore into a state of intense excitement by their near approach— had cut the northern central railroad & burned Hagerstown. These reports have all been confirmed but there are various conflicting opinions entertained in regard to the supposed object of the enemy whether a raid, merely for purposes of plunder, or a demonstration on Wash. to call off Gen. Grant's troops from the vicinity of Petersburg is still a matter of conjecture. The quartermaster's clerks have all been ordered to report themselves for service in the defence of the city.

July 11th Monday.

The city [is] in a state of intense excitement. Southerners [are] said to be at Rockville & skirmishing with our pickets. After cutting the Northern central R.R. yesterday, they proceeded across the country cutting the telegraph wires on the Phil & Harford turnpike & burning the residence of Gov. Bradford about 5 miles from Baltimore—this was in retaliation for the burning of Gov. Fletcher's house by Gen. Hunter. At Magnolia Station about 18 miles from Baltimore the bridge over Gunpowder Creek has been destroyed.

2 P.M. Mother just in from a shopping expedition. Says we are surrounded by the rebels—city filled with refugees from the country, coming in with wagons filled with household effects. Rebels fighting at Tenally Town.

4 P.M. Mr. Gill brings news of the closer approach of the enemy. Mr. Shaw has come to offer his services in case they may be needed in the defence of the Inst. Says the rebels are attacking Fort Mass. on Seventh St. We are going to the top of the high tower.

(Top of the Tower) The city lies before us peaceful & beautiful in the rays of the setting sun. The broad river lost in the distance by a cloud of mist hanging low on the horizon is dotted here & there with boats, two of which have moved with stealthy eager motion into the port of the Arsenal. We are told they are laden with troops. Dr. Hamlin & others have joined us. A jet of smoke rises curling off into the rose colored clouds, disappearing & appearing again marks the scene of the conflict if there is any. Mr. De Rust who is looking through the glass reports signals from the top of the Soldier's Home. We look & see the signal maker with his flag. A body of colored troops are moving down 12th. We watch them as they move slowly along, their wives & little ones crowding the pavements. The sun is sinking lower now & shedding its last beams over a scene of such quiet beauty it seems to mock our excitement. The shadows of the towers stretch longer & longer over green pasture below us. Gen. Hamlin tells now if tonight will the attack be made. Our hearts beat quicker. We look towards the distant Capitol, the White House & wonder if it is possible they can be in danger. But the little jets of smoke curl up lazily as before. The sun has gone down. Gen. Hamlin rises to go; we follow one by one.

In Early April

KATE DiCAMILLO

illustrated by
CHRIS SHEBAN

In early April, just before Richmond fell,
President Lincoln dreamt one night of wandering
through the White House and hearing everywhere,
in every room, the sound of weeping,
great sorrowful sobbing.
In the East Room, he came upon a dead man,
guarded by a soldier.
"Who is dead?" Lincoln said.
"Who is dead in the White House?"
The soldier said, "The president
is dead, killed by an assassin."
Lincoln awoke, shaking and afraid.

That same spring, a few nights later,
Lincoln dreamt again of dying.
He entered the White House,
and Willie was standing at the door,
waiting for him.
"Take off your hat, Pa," said Willie.
"But son," said Lincoln, "you're dead."
"Take off your hat, take off your hat," sang Willie.
The president did as his son commanded
and removed his hat and was astounded to see
butterflies
rising up out of it.
"See?" said Willie, and he laughed,
and then he slipped his hand into his father's.
The president stood with his hat in one hand,
and with the other hand he held on to his son,
and they watched the butterflies rise
out of the hat,
up into the late afternoon light.
And President Lincoln said to his son,
   "It is not, after all,
such a terrible thing to die."

On the evening that he was shot,
on his way to the theater, the president
found, on the floor of the East Room,
the wing of a butterfly.
He bent and picked it up and put it in his pocket.
At the theater, he sat and held his wife's hand.
With the other hand, he reached into his pocket
and touched, over and over again,
the wing of the butterfly.
The wing filled him
with light and peace
and thoughts of Willie,
and so he was not afraid,
not afraid at all,
when the assassin's bullet entered him.

PART IV

ONE LAMP LIGHTS ANOTHER

ILLUSTRATION BY
NANCY CARPENTER

Mrs. Cleveland, White House Bride

⌒ JENNIFER ARMSTRONG ⌒

MR. AND MRS. OSCAR FOLSOM of Buffalo, New York, had a daughter named Frank, in honor of an uncle. When Frank was a baby, her father's law partner bought her a baby carriage. And when Frank's father passed away, this partner remained a close friend of the Folsom family, helping with advice and counsel throughout Frank's years at college.

This family friend had entered politics by that time, first becoming governor of New York and finally, in 1885, winning the White House as the country's twenty-second president, Grover Cleveland. A bachelor, Cleveland invited his sister to be the White House hostess. When Frank and her mother visited the new president, the press began to suspect that there might be more than friendship between the president and the Folsom family.

Parlors from Boston to Los Angeles buzzed with the news: Mrs. Folsom, accompanied by her daughter (now called Frances), is on her way to Europe, and it can only mean one thing! Mrs. Folsom is off to buy herself a whole new wardrobe, something suitable for a First Lady. A White House wedding! In the history of the country, no president had ever been married while in office. It was like a ladies' novel, a sentimental ballad, a valentine poem on rose-scented paper! The widow marrying her late husband's partner, the gentleman who had been the two stranded females' staunchest friend and most trusted adviser for all these years—how romantic!

But the country was in for a surprise. It wasn't *Mrs.* Folsom engaged to marry the president. It was the beautiful *Frances,* tall and graceful, with blue eyes and chestnut hair. And those weren't her only beauties, for she was also blessed with wit, charm, style, and intellect! The Cleveland White House would be the most fashionable in the nation's history.

Never mind what the president was doing as leader of the country. Americans wanted all the details of the upcoming wedding, marked on calendars around the nation for June 2, 1886. How many guests would there be? Who would get a coveted invitation? What would the gown look like, and what would be served at the bridal feast? Those hoping for a great gala event were disappointed, however, when the couple announced that they would be wed in a small, private ceremony. The guest list was limited to thirty-one family members, close friends, and cabinet officials and their wives. The press was barred from entry.

Promptly at seven o'clock, President Cleveland and Frances Folsom walked into the Blue Room of the White House while John Philip Sousa led the Marine Band in the wedding march. The Blue Room had been blanketed with June flowers, but the most dazzling sight was Frances herself. The minister of the First Presbyterian Church in Washington performed his official duty toward the president and his bride, and Frank Folsom Cleveland became the first—and only—First Lady to marry the man who'd pushed her in her baby carriage.

Seven from Ohio
(For Some Reason)

written and illustrated by
NATALIE BABBITT

IT'S PRETTY MUCH IMPOSSIBLE TO SAY exactly why one person gets elected president instead of some other person who tried just as hard. So it's also pretty much impossible to say why, out of the forty-three presidents we've had so far, seven were born in Ohio. I was born in Ohio myself, and so was all my family, going back a very long way, but I don't know why so many presidents came from there. My parents didn't seem to have noticed, and nobody mentioned it at school.

The thing is, we have fifty states in America, but there weren't any presidents at all born in thirty of them, and of the other twenty states, most produced only one. But here's modest old Ohio with seven, the second-largest number after elegant Virginia's eight. Not only that, but Ohio's seven were all scrunched together in a pretty short period of time, and they were all Republicans. And not only *that*, but their wives were all born in Ohio, too, except for Mrs. Grant.

ULYSSES S. GRANT was the first Ohio president. He was our eighteenth president, elected in 1868. Everyone agrees he was a great general in the Civil War, but they say he wasn't a very good president. He seems to have let a lot of bad rich people take advantage of him. And anyway, he didn't like being president and was glad when it was over.

Next came RUTHERFORD B. HAYES, our nineteenth president, who was also a general in the Civil War. His run for president was so tight that it had to be decided by Congress, where he won by just one vote. He did a lot of good things as president; he was big on education and civil rights and tried, too, to reunite the nation after the war. But even so, no one thinks about him very much now.

Right after Hayes came JAMES A. GARFIELD, our twentieth president, who took office in 1881. He was a preacher and a teacher and then another of the Civil War generals, but he came out of all that only to get assassinated by what we call a "disappointed office seeker" when he'd been president for only four months. So he didn't have much of a chance to show what he could do.

BENJAMIN HARRISON was next, after two others who weren't born in Ohio. Harrison was our twenty-third president and was the grandson of our ninth, William Henry Harrison, who, by the way, was born in Virginia, but never mind that. Benjamin, who'd held a few political positions before he ran for president, did a lot of good things while he was in office, a time when the nation was moving away from farming and into big business. But he only served one term and afterward went back to being a lawyer.

In 1897, WILLIAM McKINLEY became the twenty-fifth president. McKinley was in office during the Spanish-American War, which helped Cuba get its independence from Spain. He was elected for a second term, but very soon afterward, he was shot in the stomach by a man who, so far as we know, doesn't seem to have had any particular motivation. McKinley died eight days later because of inadequate medical care.

Then, in 1909, WILLIAM HOWARD TAFT became president number twenty-seven. While Taft was president, the income tax came into being, and he also worked hard on antitrust suits. After he left office, he became chief justice of the Supreme Court. He was a very large man, weighing more than three hundred pounds.

WARREN G. HARDING, Ohio's last president—so far—took over in 1921 and was our twenty-ninth. This was after the end of World War I, and Harding wanted everything to be peaceful and quiet again. He had bad luck with his advisers, though, and then, in 1923, before his term of office was over, he died very suddenly.

None of Ohio's presidents was especially famous; at least not like Washington or Lincoln. It's not easy to be a president, though. A lot can go wrong, no matter how hard you try to do it right. And assassinations do happen sometimes. Of the four American presidents who have been assassinated, half were from Ohio. Still, here we have an average-sized state, out in the Midwest, minding its own business, and not very famous, either, if you're talking about a good place for honeymoons or fancy vacations. It hasn't got oceans, it's flat, and the weather is pretty much ordinary. And yet Ohio has a lot to be proud of, being the birthplace of so many presidents, even if nobody knows exactly why it happened. After all, there haven't been any presidents at all born in far-more-glamorous Florida.

THE EYES AND EARS OF THE PUBLIC

★★KATHERINE PATERSON★★
ILLUSTRATED BY ANDRÉA WESSON

Most people who work in the White House are there to serve the president, but there is one group of men and women who are there to serve us—the public. They are the White House press corps. They are there every day, ensconced in the West Wing, questioning everything that goes on in that great house and rushing to report it to the world. It is hard for any of us to like someone who is always sticking his nose into our business and then broadcasting it to the neighbors. It's not difficult to understand, then, why the president has a hard time loving the White House press corps. It might be a little bit harder to understand how they got into the White House in the first place. Wasn't the White House supposed to be the president's home?

In the early days, there were no reporters in the West Wing. Mary Clemmer Ames, who, during the 1860s, was sending letters to her local newspaper about what was going on in Washington, went into the White House only by invitation. Still, that didn't keep her from making forthright comments on the family that lived there. Not even President Grant's party-loving teenage daughter escaped her judgment. Ellen Grant would probably have gotten a lot of sympathy from every succeeding child who had to grow up in the White House under the noses of the press.

So how did those noses get into the White House itself? They were invited in. In the beginning, reporters stood outside the gates in all weather, trying to buttonhole people going in and out to get news of what was happening inside. By 1900, President McKinley realized that there were so many reporters hanging around the gates that he sent an aide out to give them a daily briefing. When Theodore Roosevelt became president, after McKinley's assassination, he liked to talk to reporters himself, chatting with those he liked and snubbing those he thought had written or might write an unfavorable story. Still, it was the first President Roosevelt who can be blamed for the creation of the press head-quarters inside the West Wing that harbors reporters of every stripe. As Helen Thomas, the most famous White House correspondent of all time, retells the story, "On a cold, rainy day in 1902, he saw the drenched reporters huddled beneath the trees on the North Lawn and invited them in. They never left."

Ms. Thomas, who for many years sat in the front row of the press corps in a bright red suit, has become such a fixture in televised presidential news conferences that some might think she dates back to Teddy Roosevelt's time. Actually, however, she came to Washington as a reporter during World War II. Her early White House experience con-sisted of covering the First Lady, a job considered suitable for a female correspondent in those days. But Eleanor Roosevelt was every bit as interesting as her husband and often broke news to the women of the press in the East Wing that the men in the West Wing had not yet heard. After Ms. Thomas stood for days in the rain (reporters still do that) to get news about the birth of John Kennedy Jr. at Georgetown Hospital, United Press International moved her inside the West Wing, where she has covered presidents and their families from Kennedy through George W. Bush. She was the only woman news-paper reporter to accompany President Nixon on his history-making trip to China. She has traveled all over the world with presidents Nixon, Ford, Carter, Reagan, George H. W. Bush, Clinton, and George W. Bush.

Thomas has always been known for her sharp questioning in the pressroom and has been critical of her fellow reporters for not being "probing enough." She feels strongly that it is the duty of the press to ask the president and his press secretary hard questions—the ones they least want to answer.

Some days presidents and their wives have loved her, and some days they have hated her, but they could never ignore the woman in red who usually had a seat on Air Force One and stood in whatever weather she had to for as long as necessary to get the story for the American people.

The press, however, is not only the public's eyes and ears in the White House, it is also, in a vital way, the mouth of the American people speaking to the president's ears. Harry Truman, who got as angry with the press as any president before or since, was still wise enough to know and express the president's need for the press. "For eight years," he told the White House correspondents, "you and I have been helping each other. I have been trying to keep you informed of the news from the point of view of the presidency. You, more than you realize, have been giving me a great deal of what the people of this country are thinking about."

Every president has tried to manage the news, to get reporters to make him look good to the American people. But in that pressroom in the West Wing, the American people have allies whose job it is to ferret out the truth of what's happening inside the White House—and also to let the president know the truth of what is going on outside its gates, in the minds and hearts of the people he has been elected to serve.

Theodore Roosevelt's Letters to His Children

LEONARD S. MARCUS

THEODORE ROOSEVELT LIVED FOR ACTION. Wellborn but physically frail, Roosevelt overcame early illness to lead a cavalry regiment in the Spanish-American War, win the admiration of leathernecked frontiersmen and the grudging respect of America's most powerful businessmen, preside over the creation of our national park system and the construction of the monumental Panama Canal, and make peace between two of the world's bitterest rival nations, Russia and Japan. Believing that life was a struggle that should also be a joy, he found many chances along the path of duty to have great fun — riding, swimming, rock climbing, bird-watching, boxing, hunting, or just "playing bear" with his children. When on a presidential hunting trip he refused to shoot a real bear that was too old to defend itself, the press reported the story as proof of his sense of fair play. Soon afterward, a new children's toy — the "teddy bear" — made its appearance in stores and became a sensation.

Roosevelt approached reading and writing as forms of action. He had devoured books as a housebound child. As president he still often read a book a day. The more than thirty-five books that he himself wrote — the most by far of any American president — span a breathtaking range from biography, natural history, and memoir to politics, literary criticism, and philosophy. Somehow, he also found the time to write more than 150,000 letters, including scores of letters to his six children. Some of these last he enlivened with his own comical drawings.

When the older children were traveling or away at school, Roosevelt delighted in writing to them about their younger siblings' latest activities. To Kermit, at Groton, he reported in January 1903, "It is just after lunch and . . . I left Mother lying on the sofa and reading aloud to Quentin, who as usual has hung himself over the back of the sofa in what I should personally regard as an exceedingly uncomfortable attitude to listen to literature." Three years later, as Kermit approached manhood, Roosevelt waxed nostalgic about the younger children's lingering attachment to make-believe: "What a heavenly place a sand-box is for two little boys! Archie and Quentin play industriously in it during most of their spare moments when out in the [White House] grounds. I often look out the windows when I have a score of Senators and Congressmen with me and see them both hard at work arranging caverns or mountains, with runways for their marbles."

At the time he wrote this, Roosevelt was about to move mountains of his own. After years of political wrangling and debate among the nation's leading engineers, final plans for the construction of the Panama Canal had at last been laid. Yet Roosevelt never forgot the limits of his power to control events. Soon after helping to bring about an end to war between Japan and Russia—an effort for which Roosevelt won the Nobel Peace Prize—he wrote Alice, "It is enough to give anyone a sense of sardonic amusement to see the way in which people . . . gauge the work purely by the fact that it succeeded. If I had not brought about peace I should have been laughed at and condemned. Now I am over-praised."

Roosevelt loved living in the White House. On June 21, 1904, on the eve of his nomination for a first full term as president, he wrote Kermit that he could not predict the outcome of the upcoming general election. Still, he added, whether he won or lost, he would always be grateful for the experience of the last three years.

Roosevelt won the election of 1904 handily. Not quite four years later, with most of official Washington and his own family already gone for the summer, Roosevelt chose to stay on for a time in the oppressively hot capital city to attend to business. Only ten-year-old Quentin, his beloved youngest child, had remained behind to keep him company. In a letter to Ted, the president confided, "Until Quentin goes to bed the house is entirely lively. After that the rooms seem big and lonely and full of echoes." To Roosevelt's regret, Quentin now considered himself too grown-up to be read to at bedtime.

Roosevelt completed his term and on March 4, 1909, turned over the presidency to his handpicked successor, William Howard Taft. He later regretted his decision not to run for reelection, but his attempt to regain the presidency in 1912 as a third-party candidate fizzled. He spent much of the remaining years of his life reading, writing, and hunting big game.

Quentin, who was eleven when his father left the White House, followed his brothers to Groton and Harvard and then, after the United States entered the Great War in 1917, into the military. Ever the adventurer, he chose one of the most dangerous of all combat assignments for himself, serving as an airman. On July 14, 1918, he died when his plane was shot down behind enemy lines in Germany. He was twenty years old.

Roosevelt was heartbroken. In the months that followed, he and a journalist friend, Joseph Bucklin Bishop, gathered material for a book to be published in 1919 as *Theodore Roosevelt's Letters to His Children*. He did not live to hold the book in hand. In the early hours of January 6, 1919, Theodore Roosevelt died suddenly of a blood clot to the lung at his home in Oyster Bay, New York. Later that year, when the *Letters* appeared, readers embraced the collection as a memorial to the father as much as to the son.

In his introduction to the volume, Bishop recalled a remark by the former president, who had led such an extraordinary, accomplished life, about the book's meaning for him. He wished, Roosevelt had told his old friend, to be remembered as the *Letters'* author: "I would rather have this book published than anything that has been written about me."

TR's Family & Friends
ILLUSTRATION BY
Chris Van Dusen

Storming Down the Stairs

Albert Marrin

The White House knew untrammeled joys
That shamed its customs prim and starchy,
When cataracts of little boys
Came storming down the stairs with Archie.
—ARTHUR GUITERMAN, circa 1908

FROM SEPTEMBER 1901 TO MARCH 1909, Theodore Roosevelt and his family lived happily and vigorously, noisily and lovingly, in the White House. The First Family had a "bully" time there, to borrow one of the president's favorite words. "I do not think that any two people ever got more enjoyment out of the White House than Mother and I," he wrote. "We love the house itself." And the Roosevelts made it their own, shaping their experience there to meet their family's needs.

When the Roosevelts first moved in, they found the White House a dark, dismal place with heavy, ornate furniture and soot-darkened ceilings. "It's like living over the store," complained the First Lady, Edith Kermit Carow Roosevelt. The space on the second floor, directly over the East Room, held offices separated from the living area by a glass screen. Pleading cramped space and lack of privacy, in 1902 "TR" got Congress to appropriate

$540,000 to enlarge, remodel, and rid the mansion (mostly) of rats, a plague since the time of John Adams. The old offices in the East Wing became bedrooms, and the West Wing was built for the clerks. Pleased with the results, TR officially changed the name from the "Executive Mansion" to the "White House."

Never had so many children called the White House home. The Roosevelts had five children of their own and a sixth older daughter, Alice, Roosevelt's child by his first wife. TR, who disliked the nickname Teddy, believed that children's "animal spirits" should be given free rein. And, indeed, the White House itself became something of a zoo extension, thanks to the children.

Pets were everywhere. Tom Quartz, usually a mild-mannered cat, took a hissing, scratching dislike to House Speaker "Uncle" Joe Cannon. There were the dogs, like Jack the terrier and Sailor Boy the retriever; the hens, Baron Speckle and Fierce; and an assortment of rabbits, flying squirrels, and kangaroo rats. The president thought Jonathan, a piebald rat, was a cuddly darling, "who crawls all over everybody," he said. Eli, the most gorgeous macaw, had "a bill that I think could bite through boiler plate" but endeared himself by screeching "Hurrah for Roosevelt!" There were horses on the grounds as well. Young Quentin once took his brother Archie's favorite Shetland pony, Algonquin, upstairs in the elevator to visit Archie when he was sick in bed.

The children also liked snakes. When Alice stayed at the White House, she went about with Emily Spinach, a long, lean snake named after her aunt, a long, lean woman named Emily Carow. Quentin adored his four-foot king snake. One day, he burst into his father's office, proudly plunking it down on the desk. Yes, TR said, such a snake was truly worthy of a boy. But since the president was in conference with the attorney general at the time, he asked Quentin to show it to some congressmen waiting in the next room. The whiskered gentlemen mistook it for a stick, until it began to move. "Then the snake went up Quentin's sleeve," TR recalled. "The last I saw of Quentin, one congressman was gingerly helping him off with his jacket, so as to let the snake crawl out of the upper end of the sleeve."

At heart, Theodore Roosevelt remained a child himself all his life. "You must always remember," joked his friend Cecil Spring Rice, the British ambassador, "that the president is about six."

EXECUTIVE ORDER FOR NATURE

Jean Craighead George

THE MOVEMENT TO PRESERVE America's revered hills, forests, water-ways, and clear blue skies began in the White House.

In 1864, when ecologist George Perkins Marsh wrote *Man and Nature,* he sounded a national alarm. He warned that deforested slopes were becoming gutters and that springs were drying up. When it rained, he wrote, streams became muddy torrents, and during dry periods, they were reduced to gravel beds. Rivers had become oceans, then deserts. Marsh warned that we must stop abusing nature or suffer the consequences.

President Theodore Roosevelt (1901–1909), wilderness lover and outdoorsman, heard Marsh's cry. When Roosevelt became president, he urged Congress to pass legislation protecting the incredible natural resources of America. When it failed to act, he lifted his fist and issued an executive order, a tool that gave presidents the power to move ahead on issues that could be settled no other way. With this tool, he established the National Wildlife Refuge System in 1903 and designated Pelican Island in Florida as its first unit.

Then he doubled the number of parks and reserves and cajoled Congress into creating the Forest Service, a group of scientifically trained men and women who would oversee and protect our forests and the land beneath them for the generations ahead.

Since that time, White House executive orders have been used to save wetlands, create marine sanctuaries, and protect Indian sacred sites, endangered species, coral reefs, western canyons, and the Arctic wilderness. The power has not been used exclusively for preservation. It has also established equality and justice in the military and in poor and minority populations. However, what one president orders, the next can undo, and many have done so. Yet today most of the environmental executive orders still stand, keeping America beautiful, healthy, and prosperous.

Love of nature lies deep in the American psyche. We inherited a wilderness, and deep in our hearts, we long to maintain its dreamlike diversity from "sea to shining sea." Said a voter in the Bronx, New York, "I may never see a grizzly bear or a giant redwood tree. I just want to know they are there."

It is the White House where the fountainhead of the preservation movement erupted into a benevolent geyser—the conservation movement. How has it gone so wrong?

AMERICA'S WILDERNESS
ILLUSTRATION BY
DAVID SLONIM

William Howard Taft

PRESIDENT, 1909–1913

Virginia Euwer Wolff

illustrated by

Kevin Hawkes

THE MARINE ORCHESTRA and the Marine String Quartet often played during White House dinners preceding the "Lenten Musicales" hosted by First Lady Helen Taft. She was a pianist who practiced every day and was one of the founders of the Cincinnati Symphony. For the musicales, Mrs. Taft selected mostly women pianists, including Olga Samaroff, Yolanda Mero, and Fannie Bloomfield Zeisler. Viennese violinist Fritz Kreisler also played for the First Family and their guests. President Taft owned a Stradivarius violin; it has since been sold, auctioned by Christie's auction house, and as of 2004 was on loan by a private owner to a young university student violinist. Taft himself listened to records on his graphonola (an early phonograph). His favorite recordings were of the tenor Enrico Caruso singing from Puccini operas and of Irving Berlin's "Alexander's Ragtime Band."

PART V

WITH COURAGE
AND
DETERMINATION

ESIDENT
WHAT
WILL YOU DO
FOR
WOMAN SUFFRAGE

ILLUSTRATION BY
EMILY ARNOLD MCCULLY

EYEWITNESS TO HISTORY

dialogue imagined by STEPHANIE S. TOLAN

JANE ROGERS: Welcome to *Eyewitness to History*, the program that travels through time to let you witness the major events of the past. The date is Monday, January 8th, 1917, and the place is Washington, D.C. I am standing on Pennsylvania Avenue, in front of the White House, where, in spite of the cold, women have been picketing daily for more than a week, demanding the right to vote. Inside, President Woodrow Wilson has refused any further meetings with the suffragettes—excuse me—they prefer to be called *suffragists*. Here with me is Alice Paul, one of the founders of the National Woman's Party and the organizer of this demonstration. Miss Paul, why have you chosen to picket the White House?

ALICE PAUL: To get the president's attention. For years, women have been working in the states and territories to secure the right to vote. But a constitutional amendment is essential if we are to make changes across the nation. Thus far the president has refused to support a suffrage amendment. We intend to change his mind.

JANE: And you think picketing will do that?

ALICE: Nothing else has done so. Four years ago, on March 3rd, 1913, the day before his inauguration, five thousand women—*five thousand!*—marched on the streets of Washington to demand the vote. Many of us were beaten and assaulted that day, because the police refused to protect the marchers. In spite of the uproar, the president ignored us. On March 17th, I personally met with him to ask where he stood on the issue. He said he had not yet made up his mind. Perhaps the continued presence of our Silent Sentinels will help him do that.

JANE: No one has ever picketed the White House before. Isn't this a pretty radical tactic?

ALICE: Of course it's radical. Radical action is what's needed. Every time the president looks out his window, he will see women standing at his very gate, demanding their rights. He will not be able to ignore that!

JANE: It's very cold to be standing outside all day, isn't it?

ALICE: Yesterday the president sent someone out to invite us in for tea by the fire. We declined. Tea! We shall build watch fires of our own right here.

JANE: How long do you plan to keep this up?

ALICE: Until our demands are met. Women will be here every day, rain or shine, heat or cold. President Wilson must understand that we will never give up. Now, if you'll excuse me, I need to return to our vigil.

JANE: There you have it, viewers, from the organizer herself. I see two pedestrians coming down Pennsylvania Avenue now. Let's see what the man and woman on the street have to say about Miss Paul's mission. Excuse me—sir? Madam? May I ask the two of you what you think about the idea that women should be given the vote?

MAN: Stuff and nonsense! Everyone knows women haven't the brain for it. Women are suited to keeping a home, raising children. They need to know their place and stay there.

JANE: And you, madam?

WOMAN: I'll tell you what would happen if women got involved in politics. They would stop getting married—that's what would happen. They would stop having children. Why, the human race would die out! All you suffragettes are a disgrace to womanhood!

JANE: Thank you. Thank you. Don't let me detain you further. Well, viewers, as you can see, not everyone agrees with Miss Paul. Let's give her a chance to respond. Miss Paul, you graduated from Swarthmore College, attended the University of Birmingham and the London School of Economics in England, and have both a master's degree in sociology and a Ph.D. in political science from the University of Pennsylvania. What do you say to men who think women don't have the brain for voting?

ALICE: I would suggest that they themselves are proof that having the right to vote does not depend on having much of a brain.

JANE: You've just been called a disgrace to womanhood. Your National Woman's Party claims it wants to give women a voice in their own lives. What if they use that voice to disagree with you?

ALICE: Our intention is to provide women with the right to vote, not to tell them what to do with it. That is, after all, the whole point of democracy.

JANE: Thank you, Alice Paul; it has been a pleasure speaking with you. And now, viewers, as we return to our studios, we remind you that women won the vote in 1920 and the human race has somehow managed to survive since then.

You may be interested to know that this first instance of picketing the White House did not go unchallenged. In July 1917, the picketers were arrested on charges of obstructing traffic. Alice Paul was among the women convicted and sent to prison, where she began a protest hunger strike. She was eventually moved to a psychiatric ward, where she was force-fed.

Whether Miss Paul's picketing ultimately helped or hurt the campaign to get women the vote, she certainly started a trend. Over the years since then, demonstrators have continued to follow her lead, picketing the White House to draw attention to their issues and make their wishes known.

This is Jane Rogers, in Washington, for *Eyewitness to History*. See you next week in another place and another time.

Woodrow Wilson's Work Without End

. . .

story by JEANNINE ATKINS

illustrated by JERRY PINKNEY

A SPRING BREEZE SWAYED LANTERNS hung from the White House pillars. Woodrow Wilson sat before his typewriter on the south portico. During his years as a professor, governor, and president, he had written many speeches, but no words came easily that night.

Edith Wilson brought him a glass of milk and a plate of crackers. "Shouldn't you get some rest?" she asked.

"Not yet." He squeezed his wife's hand, rubbed his eyes, and started typing.

A few days later, on April 6, 1917, he announced that Americans would fight in the Great War in Europe. Members of Congress cheered. When his speech was over, Woodrow Wilson went home, put his head on his desk, and cried.

Soon, more than two million soldiers sailed to battlefields in France. Life changed in American homes, too. Since the men who'd mowed the White House lawn had joined the army, a flock of sheep nibbled the grass. On wheatless Mondays, the president and his family skipped toast and sandwiches so that bread could be sent to hungry people overseas.

No chicken or steak was served in the White House on meatless Tuesdays. Automobiles were kept off the streets on Sundays to save gasoline. The First Lady sewed four dozen pairs of pajamas, sheets, and pillowcases to send to hospitals. Edith Wilson also memorized secret codes and typed letters for the president, who was busy not only with the war but also tending to railroad and streetcar workers who demanded better pay. He tried to stop lynchings in the South and to figure out what to do about the women picketing the White House gates with banners saying, VOTES FOR WOMEN!

On November 11, 1918, a treaty was signed to end the Great War. People danced in the streets, and forty-eight bonfires blazed between the White House and the Potomac River. But the president didn't have time to celebrate. He wanted to keep such a big and terrible war from happening again.

Woodrow and Edith Wilson sailed to France. People tossed violets and roses to welcome the first president to cross the Atlantic while in office. Woodrow Wilson met with British and French premiers, Indian maharajas, and Arabian emirs to discuss ways to prevent wars. After months of meetings that often began before dawn and lasted past midnight, leaders signed a treaty that set up a League of Nations. Its mission was to help countries settle arguments without guns and battles. Now Woodrow Wilson needed to convince Americans to join.

The president and First Lady returned to Washington. "Why don't you get some rest now?" Edith asked.

"Not yet," Woodrow Wilson said.

A train took them through the Midwest and Rocky Mountains and along the Pacific Coast. President Wilson told people that just as an ocean touches more than one shore, problems in Europe were problems for our nation, too. As he spoke, Edith held her hand against his back to make sure the tired man didn't fall.

Angry people who were out of work said, "Let's worry about our own country."

Others wanted to have fun now that the war was over. "Why should we care about problems in Europe?" they asked.

The president grew sad because it seemed that Americans wouldn't vote to join the League of Nations. His eyes twitched. His hands trembled. His headaches lasted all day.

Three days after returning to the White House, Woodrow Wilson fell on the bathroom floor. Edith dragged him to the Lincoln bed. The president couldn't move his left leg, left arm, or the left side of his mouth.

"Get some rest," Edith said.

The very ill president didn't argue.

During the following months, few except his wife and doctor saw Woodrow Wilson. After he was able to sit up, rugs were put away into storage so that his wheelchair could roll more easily. Edith read him newspaper headlines and sometimes whole articles. When congressmen came by, she decided what questions he should be asked. Some people said that Edith Wilson should be called Mrs. President. She insisted that she didn't make decisions but only interpreted those made by her husband.

At the end of two terms in office, Woodrow and Edith Wilson quietly left the White House. They moved across town to a house where Woodrow Wilson died three years later. The National Cathedral was filled with mourners for the only president who has ever been buried in Washington, D.C. Decades passed and a second world war was fought before some of his ideas about peace between countries were used to form the United Nations.

Hoover's One Term
Matt Phelan

1931: President Hoover has been in office for three years. . . .

On October 24, 1929, the biggest stock market crash in history began the Great Depression.

Millions lost their jobs. Breadlines and soup kitchens were common across the nation.

Many people also lost their homes. Makeshift communities of tents and shacks were built in parks near railroad tracks.

People called these tent cities Hoovervilles.

But President Hoover believed that there was no need for alarm. Certainly with trade and tariff changes, the economy would eventually get back on track.

CRUNCH.

Soon, in cities like New York, apple peddlers were working on many street corners. They sold apples for five cents each, earning only a few pennies per apple—not much of a living.

Despite the suffering of the people, President Hoover stayed his course. He truly believed that the poor would get by without federal government intervention.

Years later, Herbert Hoover would write in his memoirs that "many persons left their jobs for the more profitable one of selling apples."

President Hoover did not get the chance to see if his plan of nonintervention would end the Depression.

In 1932, he lost the presidential election to Franklin Delano Roosevelt.

President Roosevelt's plan to end the Depression—known as the New Deal—included many federally supported work and relief programs for the unemployed.

A RAINMAKER
IN THE
WHITE HOUSE

· · ·

MICHAEL COOPER

WAS IT JUST A COINCIDENCE? Or did President Franklin D. Roosevelt, the man who lived in the White House from 1933 to 1945, actually bring rain to the Great Plains during one of the worst droughts in history?

The Great Plains are a broad swath of prairie stretching across thirteen states, from the Rocky Mountains east to the Mississippi Valley, from southern Texas up through North Dakota and far into Canada. In the 1930s, years of hot weather and excessive farming created a long drought in the region, which journalists dubbed the Dust Bowl.

This drought occurred during the decade-long economic crisis of the Great Depression. The Depression was the worst threat America had faced since the Civil War. So people on the Great Plains had to suffer through the dual disasters of depression and drought.

Rivers and wells ran dry; the soil hardened and cracked; crops withered and died. The winds that regularly swept across the prairie gathered the dry dirt and carried it away, creating dust storms that were called black blizzards. "We were," said one man, "burned out, blown out, and starved out."

No one had ever witnessed such a severe environmental problem. The drought and blowing sand turned 150,000 square miles of farm- and ranchland into "a picture of complete destruction," observed one government official. The Dust Bowl was a big, festering sore on the nation's midsection.

Many people sent suggestions to President Roosevelt at the White House on how to keep the Great Plains from blowing away.

One North Carolina woman suggested scattering old cars across the prairie; the junked autos would hold the soil down.

A man recommended paving over the entire region with concrete, leaving lots of holes for planting wheat and other seeds.

A Chicago paper company suggested covering the prairie with tough paper.

President Roosevelt had his own plans for helping people escape the poverty caused by depression, drought, and dust. He put tens of thousands of farmers to work building roads, bridges, schools, parks, and other public facilities. And the president paid farmers not to raise so much wheat and cotton so that overproduction would not keep prices low. The money helped feed starving people and kept them from becoming homeless or joining the growing army of migrant farmworkers in California.

But the millions of dollars that Roosevelt sent to the Great Plains did not end the drought. That didn't happen until he paid a visit to the plains.

In 1938, the president traveled by train to Amarillo, Texas. His visit thrilled the city's residents. Thousands of cheering people filled the streets. A huge marching band, said to be the largest ever assembled, welcomed the popular president.

As Roosevelt spoke, something happened that made people suspect he might have connections beyond Washington, D.C. Rain began to pour from the sky. No one ran for shelter. Everyone stood happily in the downpour.

The rain that returned to the region that year was the beginning of the end of the Dust Bowl. In 1941, after Roosevelt became the first and only president elected to the White House for three terms, record-breaking rains soaked the Great Plains. The long years of life-destroying drought had come to an end.

PORTRAIT OF FDR
ILLUSTRATION BY
BARRY MOSER

THE FOUR FREEDOMS

From Franklin D. Roosevelt's Address to Congress,
January 6, 1941

IN THE FUTURE DAYS, which we seek to make secure, we look forward to a world founded upon four essential human freedoms.

The first is freedom of speech and expression—everywhere in the world.

The second is freedom of every person to worship God in his own way—everywhere in the world.

The third is freedom from want, which, translated into world terms, means economic understandings which will secure to every nation a healthy peacetime life for its inhabitants—everywhere in the world.

The fourth is freedom from fear, which, translated into world terms, means a worldwide reduction of armaments to such a point and in such a thorough fashion that no nation will be in a position to commit an act of physical aggression against any neighbor—anywhere in the world.

OF SPEECH

LOUD!

ILLUSTRATION BY
CALEF BROWN

ILLUSTRATION BY
Peter Sís

FREEDOM
TO
WORSHIP

ILLUSTRATION BY
ED YOUNG

Freedom from Fear

ILLUSTRATION BY
STEPHEN ALCORN

HANDS

short story by Patricia MacLachlan

illustrated by P.J. Lynch

ELLIE MAUDE MOON STANDS in a long line of people waiting to get into the White House.

"Aren't you too warm?" Mama asks Ellie.

Ellie shakes her head. "I like to wear my jacket," she says.

Her brother, Jack, smiles at Ellie. He knows that her cat, Bitty, is hiding under the jacket. He knows Ellie didn't want to leave her cat behind at the farm. But Jack won't tell.

The line begins to move toward the gate of the White House.

"Maybe you'll get to see your hero," Papa says to Mama. "Mrs. Roosevelt is your mama's hero."

"Does she wear a crown?" asks Ellie.

"She is not a queen," says Mama.

"Does she wear a cape and fly?" asks Ellie.

"She is not that kind of hero, Ellie," says Mama. "She is a good person. She writes letters to children and takes care of the poor. She says everyone, no matter what the color of his skin, is worthy. She is very kind during these hard times."

Ellie knows about the hard times. Many people are out of work. They are poor. Some have lost their homes. Sometimes Mama feeds them. Sometimes they stay in the house, or in the barn, or in their cars. Their eyes are sad. Once a woman cried, and Mama put her arms around her.

"What does Mrs. Roosevelt look like?" asks Ellie.

"She has a wonderful smile," says Mama.

The line moves forward, and at that moment, Bitty pushes her nose out of Ellie's jacket. She squirms and jumps out of Ellie's arms.

"Bitty!" cries Ellie.

"What?" says Papa loudly. "How did she get here?"

Bitty slips between the iron bars of the fence. Ellie chases after her.

"Stop!" yells a policeman.

"Ellie! Come back!" her mama calls.

But Ellie runs after Bitty as fast as she can. Bitty, small and orange, runs across the lawn of the White House. Ellie hears more voices, people calling and running after her. She begins to cry as she runs.

"Bitty! Bitty!" Ellie calls.

The policeman runs after Ellie. "Stop!" he yells again.

Bitty jumps to a tree and begins climbing. The tree has many branches reaching out. Ellie tries to climb after her.

"Wait, child," a woman's soft voice says. "I think I can reach your friend."

Ellie nods, not speaking. She watches the woman's hands, the fingers long and graceful.

The policeman runs up, and the woman holds out her hand to stop him.

"There," she says, gently taking Bitty down from the tree. She holds Bitty against her chest. "There. Had a little run, did you? This is your cat?"

Ellie nods, not speaking. She watches the woman's hands as they stroke Bitty.

The policeman comes closer.

"It's all right, Charles. Where are your parents, dear?"

"In line, waiting to see the people's house. Waiting to see Mrs. Roosevelt. She's a hero, you know."

The woman smiles. Her smile is beautiful. Charles smiles, too.

"Charles, will you find this child's parents?" She stops. "What is your name?"

"Ellie Moon."

"Ellie," says the woman thoughtfully. "Please tell Ellie's parents that she is fine, Charles. She will catch up with them inside later."

"Yes, Mrs. —" He stops because the woman shakes her head.

"Was it a secret that you brought your cat from home?" the woman asks Ellie.

Ellie feels her face get hot.

"Her name is Bitty. I'll be in trouble," says Ellie. "How did you know?"

"I guessed," says the woman. "I bet you're an Eleanor, aren't you?"

Ellie nods.

"Well, I am an Eleanor, too," says the woman.

The woman named Eleanor hands Bitty to Ellie.

"Thank you for saving Bitty," says Ellie.

"You're welcome."

"I bet Mrs. Roosevelt would save Bitty, too," says Ellie.

"I think so," says Eleanor.

"Do you work here?" asks Ellie.

"I do."

"It's a very big place."

"It is," says Eleanor with a sigh. "Too big. Sometimes I wish for a small, serene place far away."

"That's where I live!" says Ellie happily. "You can visit me at the farm. Unless it's filled up."

"Filled up?"

"With people who have no jobs and money. Or homes," says Ellie.

Eleanor sighs again. "Yes, they need help."

"Mama and Papa help them." Ellie looks around. "You know, maybe some of them could live here. There's lots of room here."

"That's a splendid idea, Ellie. Splendid!"

Eleanor takes a piece of yarn from a basket and ties it around Bitty's neck. "This is so Bitty won't run away again. I want you to meet someone, and then we'll find your mama and papa."

Eleanor and Ellie walk across the green lawn, past the blooming bushes and the tall trees. Bitty follows them at the end of her yarn leash, jumping every so often at a leaf or a blade of grass.

They come to a stone walk around the White House. Eleanor takes Ellie's hand.

"The someone I want you to meet is just inside. He will like you," says Eleanor.

"Who is it?" asks Ellie.

"The president," says Eleanor.

Ellie stops. "*The* president of the United States?"

"That one," says Eleanor.

She knocks at a French door, and they go inside. It is a beautiful gold room—a round-shaped room.

A man sits at a large desk. He looks up and smiles when he sees Eleanor. "Well, what do we have here?" he says.

"This is a visitor. Two visitors. Ellie and Bitty."

"How do you do?" says the president.

Ellie puts out her hand and shakes the president's hand.

"Are you Bitty?" he asks, making Ellie laugh.

"This is Ellie, and you know it," says Eleanor. "Ellie supports human rights, Mr. President. And she has come up with an interesting suggestion."

"Is that so?" says the president.

"Yes. Ellie's parents have taken in many people who don't have homes or jobs. Ellie thinks our house would be a good place for people to live. She thinks we have plenty of room."

The president smiles. "Excellent idea, Ellie. In the meantime, I hope your family continues to help."

"Yes, sir," says Ellie. "I'll tell my mama and papa. Today is my mama's birthday. I'm sure she would be glad to meet you. But she really came to meet her hero, Mrs. Roosevelt. Will you please tell her that?"

"But, my dear," says the president slowly, "she already knows." He looks at Eleanor.

Ellie's eyes widen. She looks at her friend Eleanor.

* * *

Eleanor takes Ellie's hand again. They walk out of the beautiful room. They walk down a long hall with marble floors. They walk past statues and huge paintings hung high on the walls. They walk past guards in uniforms, who nod to Eleanor. Then Ellie sees Mama and Papa and Jack. She begins to walk fast, pulling Eleanor after her.

"Mama, Mama," calls Ellie, "I've come with your hero!"

Mama turns.

"You told me about her smile," says Ellie. "But you forgot to tell me about her hands!"

And then Mama sees Eleanor, carrying Bitty in her arms.

Eleanor Roosevelt smiles. "Happy birthday," she says.

A Perfect Image

LINDA SUE PARK
illustrated by STÉPHANE JORISCH

THE LEG OF A PIANO once closed down the whole White House.

In 1948, shortly after President Harry Truman had a balcony added to the south portico, a leg of his beloved Steinway piano crashed through the floor of the second-story study. It turned out that the entire building was in need of a serious overhaul. From 1948 to 1952, while the White House was being restored, the Trumans didn't even live there. They stayed at Blair House, across the street.

My parents were teenagers in Korea at around this time, before and during the Korean War. What they knew of the world outside Korea came from radio and newspapers (they had no television). Though my parents were not aware of many news events taking place in the United States at the time, they do remember the story about the Steinway— because they were surprised to learn that Truman played the piano.

A president who played the piano? It struck my parents and their compatriots as not very, well, *presidential*. Korean politicians of the time would have considered it undignified to publicize such trivia as their hobbies.

Fifty years after that White House renovation, in October of 2002, I was invited to the White House for the National Book Festival. As part of the celebration, dozens of authors of books for young people were to have breakfast with First Lady Laura Bush. Each author was allowed a guest. I invited my father and cajoled another author into bringing my mother as her guest. So both of my parents got to attend.

The crowd moved slowly into the grand Entrance and Cross Halls. It became a lively gathering—people eating and talking and standing in a ragged line to greet Mrs. Bush. By her side was the First Lady of Russia, Lyudmila Putin, who had come to the book festival with the hope of doing something similar in her country.

My parents were delighted to see a grand piano in the Entrance Hall. It was not the Truman Steinway (that one is now in the Truman Presidential Museum & Library in Independence, Missouri), but it seemed to have been plucked straight from their childhood memories of the White House.

I went to get coffee. From across the room, I saw my parents talking with Mrs. Putin.

My parents do not speak Russian. To my knowledge, Mrs. Putin does not speak Korean. How I wish I could have heard that conversation, the English flavored heavily with the spice and salt of their native languages.

My parents, Korean immigrants and naturalized U.S. citizens, chatting gaily with Russia's First Lady in front of a piano: That, to me, is a perfect image of the White House.

A Note for the President

Jerry Spinelli

illustrated by Terry Widener

IN THE SUMMER OF 1950, when I was nine, my parents told me we were taking a trip to Washington, D.C. I didn't think much of it at first. Then they said we would tour the White House. That got my attention.

The biggest problem in my life at that time had to do with a basketball net—or more precisely, the lack of one. I lived on the 800 block of George Street in Norristown, Pennsylvania. Down at the dead end was a telephone pole. Nailed to the pole, ten feet up, was a warped, chipped, unpainted plywood backboard. Nailed to the backboard was a rusty iron rim that bent downward like a drooping lower lip. This was our basketball court.

It was rumored that the rim had once had a net, and in fact an inch-long scrap of string still clung to the hoop. But none of us had ever experienced the luxury of seeing a shot of ours fall through a net. None of us had ever heard the proverbial *swish*!

Several days before our visit to the White House, I wrote a note to President Truman. I asked him for a net. I understood that the president of the United States was unlikely to climb a ladder and attach the net himself, but I was sure he could get it done. My plan was to hand the note to him at the White House.

When the day came, I was surprised at how long the line was to get in. As the guide took us from room to room, I kept an eye peeled for the president. The tour was coming to an end, and still he hadn't shown up. I asked the guide, "When do we see the president?"

She smiled. She leaned down with her hands on her knees. "We don't," she said. "He's very busy. He's in another part of the building."

This was bad news for me, and time was running out.

The last room we visited had red walls and lots of dishes. A guard was standing at one door. He wore a blue and red uniform with gold trim and white gloves, which I didn't see at first because his hands were behind his back. I went up to him. I took the folded piece of paper from my pocket. "Can I ask you something?" I said.

He looked down from his great height. His voice was softer than I expected. "Sure," he said.

I held out the note. "Could you give this to President Truman for me?"

Out came a white-gloved hand. He took the note. I was afraid he might unfold and read it, but he didn't. He put it in his front pants pocket, which my father always told me was the safest pocket of all. "I'll see that he gets it," he said.

I was about to go when it occurred to me that the grown-up thing to do would be to shake hands. "Thanks," I said. I held out my hand.

With his left hand, he began pulling on the fingers of his right glove. When it was off, he nodded and shook my hand. I turned and left.

It would be nice to report that two days later a White House carpenter showed up at the dead end of George Street and hung a gleaming white nylon net on the rusty old hoop. It did not happen. But even though we didn't get a new net, the tall sentinel had made me feel important—and I never doubted that he kept his promise.

The House Haunts

The House Haunts

M. T. Anderson

ILLUSTRATED BY MARK TEAGUE

AFTER PRESIDENT HARRY S. TRUMAN was awakened at four o'clock in the morning by a ghostly knocking on his bedroom door and the sound of footsteps in the empty hall, he told his wife, Bess, that the White House "is haunted sure as shootin'." Many others would agree.

Some say that a British soldier killed on the White House grounds during the War of 1812 still walks the lawns with a torch in his hand. Others say that a dead doorman still welcomes visitors and that a dutiful servant, though deceased, still shuts off lights at night. Some say that Abigail Adams, wife of President John Adams, bustles toward the East Room, carrying a load of laundry to be dried. When gardeners tried to dig up Dolley Madison's rose garden, she returned from the grave to tell them off—so they fled, and the garden remained. Roosevelt, Truman, and Hoover all heard Lincoln knock on their bedroom door; and when Lincoln himself was alive and well, Mrs. Lincoln heard the dead Andrew Jackson tramp up and down the corridors, swearing.

Lincoln's ghost is the most frequently seen. Winston Churchill, British prime minister during World War II, refused to stay in the Lincoln Bedroom after a disturbing sighting there. Churchill had just taken a relaxing bath with a cigar and a glass of Scotch. He stepped out of the bathroom, naked, his cigar still in his hand, to find himself confronted by the Great Emancipator, leaning on the mantelpiece.

Churchill—startled, but never at a loss for words—tapped the ash off the end of his cigar and said, "Good evening, Mr. President. You seem to have me at a disadvantage."

There is something fitting about the house of our country's leaders being inhabited by the spirit of Abraham Lincoln, a man who governed during a time of such anguish. If the White House were not haunted by the memory of its past trials, that would be a true cause for worry. As for Harry Truman, who was roused from his sleep by Lincoln's anxious knocking and pacing, he was asked whether he himself would ever return as a presidential specter. He said he wouldn't: "No man in his right mind would want to come here of his own accord."

A PRAYER FOR PEACE

From Dwight D. Eisenhower's
Farewell Address to the Nation,
January 17, 1961

WE PRAY THAT PEOPLES of all faiths, all races, all nations may have their great human needs satisfied; that those now denied opportunity shall come to enjoy it to the full; that all who yearn for freedom may experience its spiritual blessings; that those who have freedom will understand, also, its heavy responsibilities; that all who are insensitive to the needs of others will learn charity; that the scourges of poverty, disease, and ignorance will be made to disappear from the earth; and that, in the goodness of time, all peoples will come to live together in a peace guaranteed by the binding force of mutual respect and love.

Good Nights

LEE BENNETT HOPKINS

ILLUSTRATED BY WILLIAM LOW

"Good night,"

Said

An Abraham
A Mary
A Warren
A Florence
A Bess
A Harry —

Two Abigails
Four Johns
Six Jameses
One Dwight —

So many
Bade —

Still bid

"Good night" —

Through
The dark
Ebon-black —

Through
The house
That is
White.

ILLUSTRATION BY
STEVE JOHNSON AND LOU FANCHER

PART VI

THE PEOPLE'S HOUSE

THE KENNEDY WHITE HOUSE

Barbara Harrison

THE KENNEDY YEARS WERE A TIME of unparalleled excitement and exhilaration in the nation's capital. Against the backdrop of domestic and global events and crises, the stately mansion was the site of bustling family activity and festive affairs of state. President John Fitzgerald Kennedy was energetic, charming, the youngest president-elect in the history of the nation, and the first Roman Catholic to hold the office. He and his wife, Jacqueline Bouvier Kennedy, were the parents of two young children: Caroline, born November 27, 1957, and John Jr., born November 25, 1960, only two weeks after JFK was elected president. Caroline and John Jr. were the youngest children to live in the White House in more than half a century.

The children's antics were a constant source of pleasure for the president and the public. The press reported John Jr.'s first teeth, first words, first steps. When Caroline walked into a press conference wearing her mother's high-heeled shoes, the president's face lit up amid the chuckles of reporters. The children enjoyed a playground on the sprawling south lawn with tree house and swing, and Caroline attended a nursery school on the third floor of the White House. Millions of Americans came to view the Kennedys as extended family.

In an unusual move, John Kennedy had invited Robert Frost to read a poem at his inauguration, signaling his respect for the power of words and the life of the mind. To enliven interest in literature and the arts, the Kennedys held dinner gatherings featuring theatrical performances, dramatic readings, and choral and orchestral events. Guests raved about the performances. They also appreciated Mrs. Kennedy's historic restoration of the White House and the warmth and informality, yet dignity, of Kennedy hospitality.

The difficulties of his work as chief executive were great, but President Kennedy thrived under pressure, and he loved his job. He quipped to a friend, "This is the best White House I ever lived in." John Kennedy viewed the office as "the vital center of action," and radiating from this center were far-reaching concerns. No event tested his leadership more than the Cuban Missile Crisis in October 1962, a time of mounting Cold War tensions.

On the morning of October 16, the president's national security adviser interrupted him at breakfast with a sheaf of photographs indicating that the Soviet Union was installing nuclear missiles in Cuba capable of devastating the United States. Alarmed, Kennedy called to the White House top advisers (later dubbed ExComm, for Executive Committee of the National Security Council). For thirteen days, as the nation hovered on the brink of unprecedented nuclear confrontation, the executive mansion buzzed with the highest-level deliberations. The president ordered a naval blockade, and on October 28, under escalating pressure, Soviet Premier Nikita S. Khrushchev agreed to dismantle the missiles. Kennedy and ExComm heaved a collective sigh of relief. The president had acted prudently and averted disaster. Many believe it was his finest hour.

In the American people, John Fitzgerald Kennedy awakened possibilities that had long been dormant—new frontiers in space, and in economic and social justice. From the Oval Office, he gave a televised speech on civil rights that appealed to the conscience of the nation. He proposed the boldest civil rights laws in a century. From this same office, he signed the executive order that established the Peace Corps, an initiative to provide assistance to poor nations. In the nearby Treaty Room, he signed the Nuclear Test Ban Treaty, the first arms-control agreement in the nuclear age. President Kennedy inspired in his people a feeling of the nation's heroic promise and an awareness of its humane mission.

THE WHITE HOUSE, THE MOON, AND A COAL MINER'S SON

★ ★ ★

Homer Hickam
illustrated by *Joe Cepeda*

IN THE SPRING OF 1960, Senator John F. Kennedy was fighting for his political survival in the West Virginia presidential primary. He was up against Senator Hubert Humphrey, a fellow Democrat who was very popular with the coal-mining labor unions. According to the political pundits of the times, if Kennedy couldn't defeat Humphrey in West Virginia, his bid for the presidency was over.

While John Kennedy was waging his primary battles, I was a high-school senior and just gearing up for my career as a rocket builder in Coalwood, West Virginia. After being inspired by the sight of Sputnik and after three years of hard work, five other coal miners' sons and I had managed to learn how to build sophisticated rockets and send them miles into the sky. Our designs had won all the local and state science fairs, and we would soon be heading to the National Science Fair to show them what West Virginia boys could do.

The first time I ever saw then-Senator Kennedy was in April 1960, when I came across him standing on top of a Cadillac over in Welch, the county seat of McDowell County. I had come there to buy a suit to wear to the National Science Fair. The suit I had

picked was a bright orange, and I was so proud of it, I was wearing it just to show it off. Kennedy was giving a speech to a small knot of coal miners who were standing around, looking pretty listless. I immediately recognized what his problem was. The senator's audience wanted a little entertainment. Why else would they come to hear a politician after a hard day's work in the mines?

I decided to ask Senator Kennedy a question, and for some reason, he noticed me right off. My orange suit might have had something to do with it. "What do you think we ought to do in space?" I asked him, even though it wasn't a subject he'd talked about.

Kennedy looked at me for what seemed about a year and then demanded, "Well, young man, what do you think we should do in space?"

Lately, I'd been looking at the moon a lot through a telescope we Rocket Boys had set atop one of Coalwood's buildings. "We should go to the moon!" I said with such vigor that I got applause and cheers from everybody standing around.

The clapping and cheering seemed to surprise Kennedy. As if he had a sudden inspiration, he said maybe I was right, that what we needed to do was get the country moving again, and if going to the moon could help that, maybe it was just the thing. Then he asked me what we should do on the moon when we got there, and I said we should find out what it was made of and go ahead and mine the blamed thing. The miners responded with more whoops and hollers and cries that West Virginians could go and "mine that old moon good!" I got a benevolent smile from the senator.

After that, I went on to win the gold medal in the National Science Fair, and Senator Kennedy went on to win his elections in West Virginia and the entire country, too. Before I knew it, he was in the White House proposing to get the nation moving again, not only around the world but also in space. To make good on his promise, he stood up before Congress and announced, "I believe that this nation should commit itself to achieving the goal, before this decade is out, of landing a man on the moon and returning him safely to the earth."

That speech officially began the race to the moon, but I like to think we got it started down in the coalfields of West Virginia.

A WHITE HOUSE PHYSICIAN

James Young, M.D.

I WAS BORN in the farm country of Ohio and attended a school that had two rooms—one upstairs and one downstairs. By the time I reached the fifth grade and graduated to the second floor of our schoolhouse, I was convinced that I wanted to become a doctor. My father said that he and my mother would not be able to put me through college and that I would have to do it myself.

In high school, I excelled in academics and football, and this resulted in my getting offers for full scholarships to play college football. I narrowed down my choices to the schools with the best medical programs.

I attended Duke University, where I played football for four years, and afterward was drafted by the Los Angeles Rams. I was intent on being a doctor, though, so I never played professional football.

I had joined the Navy Reserve in college, and after becoming a reserve officer in medical school, I was required to serve on active duty. After completing my residency at Bethesda Naval Hospital, I was selected to be the medical officer on the 15,000-ton cruiser *Northampton,* which became the president's Command Post Afloat. Once the president was aboard, we would be available to evacuate him and his staff to safety on the ship in the event of a nuclear bomb attack. The president would then be able to run the war from the *Northampton.* The ship followed President Kennedy up and down the eastern seaboard and even to Caracas, Venezuela.

When President Kennedy came on board the *Northampton* in 1962, he had dinner with the officers and breakfast with the enlisted crew, then reviewed the entire Atlantic Fleet. Aircraft carriers, cruisers, destroyers, frigates, and submarines lined up on either side of the *Northampton,* while President Kennedy stood on the first deck, giving recognition to each passing ship.

In 1963, I was invited to become the White House physician by President Kennedy as an assistant to Captain George G. Burkley, U.S. Navy. I saw President Kennedy about once a week for minor problems and traveled in the Secret Service backup car when Mrs. Kennedy and the children visited Camp David. I wore civilian clothes to blend in with the Secret Service agents and carried a fully loaded medical bag to use in case of an emergency.

The most extreme emergency imaginable occurred when President Kennedy was shot in Dallas. I attended his eleven-hour autopsy at Bethesda Naval Hospital. I stayed with Mrs. Kennedy after her husband's death as she traveled between the White House and their summer home in Hyannis, Massachusetts. I greatly felt the loss of President Kennedy, who was a gentle, thoughtful, fun-loving, and intelligent man, but it was my honor to serve such a marvelous, kind, and considerate lady as Mrs. Kennedy.

When President Johnson took office, I remained the First Family's physician. Fortunately for my family, Lynda and Luci Johnson often included my own four children in their play. Lynda and Luci actually got into an argument about which of them would take our children for a swim in the president's pool.

During this time, I was always in immediate contact with the White House and Secret Service. I drove a White House car with a two-way radio (on which my code name was "Sunburn") and had White House telephones with direct lines to the White House switchboard in my home. I traveled many places with the Secret Service during the three years that I was doctor to the Johnsons—on USS *Sequoia,* on Air Force One, and on Marine Helicopter One.

I was able to pursue my dream thanks to drive and persistence, always setting high standards for myself, and I was rewarded with the amazing experience of working for two United States presidents. I will always be grateful for the opportunity.

A White Mouse
in the
White House

Anita Silvey

AS A YOUNG GIRL, Jackie Bouvier read with passion—books such as Kipling's Mowgli stories and Frances Hodgson Burnett's *Little Lord Fauntleroy.* She even experimented with writing and illustrating stories for her younger half-brother and half-sister. When she went to Europe in 1951, she and her sister, Lee, produced a book together, *One Special Summer,* which Jackie illustrated. Throughout her life, she felt comfortable with writers and with books.

Around 1958, before Jackie Kennedy had become First Lady, she read the book *Madeline* by Ludwig Bemelmans to her baby daughter, Caroline, and wrote him a fan letter. Bemelmans sent back a sketch of Madeline inscribed "for Jacqueline's baby," and the two began corresponding. After the Kennedys moved to the White House, Jackie continued sending letters to Bemelmans, who suggested creating a book called *Madeline Visits Caroline in the White House.* He thought that a white mouse in the White House could narrate the story. Hoping that Jackie herself would write a short text, Bemelmans even sent her a diary to record the various daily events that could serve as fodder for the story. Unfortunately, Bemelmans died in 1962, leaving the project uncompleted. Throughout her life, Jackie kept a copy of Bemelmans's last book, *On Board Noah's Ark,* inscribed "To Jackie with Love." But it would be several decades before the "dear First Lady," as Bemelmans called her, would actually collaborate on some children's books.

In 1975 Jackie Kennedy Onassis agreed to serve as an editor at Viking. She quickly took on the role of a working editor, impressing both her colleagues and her authors as a bright, talented woman with an artistic sensibility. By the time Czech illustrator Peter Sís met her many years later, she had distinguished herself as a senior editor at Doubleday. Because Sís felt it might be impolite to acknowledge her life outside of the publishing house, he treated her as if she had always been an editor—and not a former First Lady. This charade continued throughout all of their working partnership together. Jackie admired Sís's artwork and searched for the right illustration project for him. After she visited Prague, she urged him to create a book about his former home, a subject always dear to his heart. Sís—who would later become the first children's book illustrator to receive a MacArthur Foundation "genius award"—dedicated the resulting book, *The Three Golden Keys,* to her: "Thank you for a dream, J.O.!"

A multilingual former First Lady, Jackie embraced the international community in her taste in books: she owned copies of Hergé's *The Adventures of Tintin* in their original French version, and she edited *The Firebird and Other Russian Fairy Tales,* illustrated by Boris Zvorykin. As an editor she sought out material on ancient histories and other cultures, and she gravitated toward children's books that reflected a multiethnic, multicultural community.

Jackie's own advice to the young reflects her life philosophy: "Read for escape, read for adventure, read for romance, but read the great writers. You will find, to your delight, that they are easier and more joy to read than the second-rate ones."

Escape Map

Mark London Williams

WHEN I WAS GROWING UP, we were afraid that things could start blowing up around us any minute.

Does that sound familiar?

It's pretty much the kind of world grown-ups have been raising their kids in since at least the middle of the twentieth century.

Back in the '60s, we were so afraid of this "blowing up" that I drew an escape map on my bedroom wall. The map included our house, our neighbors' house, and my grandma's house, too, which seemed the best place to escape to. In those days, her home was on the edge of town, and I guess I thought I'd be safe there.

This all happened in a time—maybe like now—when no one felt very safe. At least the grown-ups didn't, and we kids could tell. It was a time called the Cold War.

The Cold War was a kind of war between America—along with its allies in Europe—and a government that doesn't exist anymore called the Soviet Union. A "cold" war is one where the shooting hasn't started yet and the two big enemies don't fight each other directly: instead, they send secret agents to spy on their opponents, and they give weapons to smaller countries, forcing them to take sides and fight each other.

The big countries watch and fight each other indirectly. It's like a video game where the bloodshed you watch from a distance turns out to be real.

Today, though, the Soviet Union has gone back to using its old name, Russia.

The Soviets had a system of beliefs and economics they called communism, where the idea was that everyone was supposed to be equal and the government owned everything. But they also had secret police, prison camps, and leaders appointed for life, and it wasn't really very equal at all. Here in the United States, we had lots of great words about freedom provided by people like Thomas Jefferson and Tom Paine and Sam Adams, but we were still trying hard to live up to them: to let everyone exercise his or her right to vote, to make sure people who weren't born rich could be equal to those who were. Of course, we did have rock and roll and blue jeans, and back in the '50s and '60s, that counted for a lot.

But we also had nuclear weapons—lots of missiles and bombs that used fission, the process of atoms splitting apart—to create huge explosions that could destroy cities, block out the sun, and leave radioactive poison around for decades after their use. Enough bombs, really, to pretty much destroy the world as we know it.

The Soviets had their own bunch of nuclear bombs, too, and the big worry during the Cold War was that all those atom-powered bombs would start going off.

That worry might have reached its peak in 1962, during an event called the Cuban Missile Crisis. That was when John F. Kennedy was in the White House, and it was discovered that the Soviet Union had put missiles in Cuba, a small country just off the coast of Florida—missiles that could get to the U.S. in just a few minutes if they were ever launched.

At this point, President Kennedy—or JFK, as everyone called him—huddled up in a secret room, the "Situation Room," in the basement of the White House, to decide what to do.

The Situation Room is a gigantic conference room, about the size of a house—or two houses, really: 5,000 square feet. The heads of different government agencies, and different generals and commanders, are all supposed to be able to meet there to exchange info and—hopefully—make wise decisions during emergencies. It had only recently been built, after an event called the Bay of Pigs invasion, where the U.S. had backed an invasion of Cuba in an attempt to overthrow its dictator, Fidel Castro, who was being supported by the Soviet Union. Castro had overthrown the previous dictator, who was supported by us. It was the "video game" thing again, but with very real consequences.

After that, JFK decided that he needed better information at his fingertips. This was before the Internet had been invented (the Internet was intially a military idea, too, so that computers could stay "hooked up" and the government could still run even if everything else was blown up). So the original Situation Room was designed to create connections—through audio and video cables—to other offices, including the Defense Department and State Department, that would allow the president to have as much instant "real-time" information as possible. This was pretty advanced for its time, in those pre-IM days. They had some of the earliest digital clocks on the wall, too, so that they could get accurate readings of the time in Washington and elsewhere.

(Recently, the Situation Room was updated, since instant information isn't nearly as hard to come by these days as it was then—although accurate information still is. But, consistent with the way secrets are kept in Washington, no one is really saying what technologies the updates included.)

Kennedy wanted his own sources of information so that he could make his own decisions, because he knew some of his generals thought the time had come to get this whole Cold War business over with and start blowing things up directly, and some of the Soviet generals felt the same way.

It was a strange idea, really: that in order to prove your point about how much better you and your country were, you'd be willing to blow up the other guys and kill huge groups of innocent people. To prove this point, you'd also be willing to see your own country destroyed in the process.

Grown-ups have a lot of peculiar ideas, and they gave a name to this one: mutually assured destruction, which, like JFK, was also known by its initials—MAD. One of the ideas behind MAD was that it might encourage the Cold War to stay cold if each side knew it could destroy the world by hitting the "launch" buttons.

But when the Cuban Missile Crisis hit, the government began handing out flyers explaining how to live in underground bomb shelters, just in case, and even how to have babies in there.

I know this because my mom was pregnant with my little sister at the time, so my parents had one of those flyers.

The Cuban Missile Crisis lasted ten days. JFK decided to try blocking off Cuba with naval ships so that no new missiles or supplies could get in. He decided not to listen to the generals who wanted to blow things up. With or without the Situation Room, we can all be thankful for that decision.

The Soviet leader at the time, a man named Khrushchev, also decided not to listen to his generals who wanted to launch their missiles. Instead, the Americans and the Soviets held a lot of secret meetings, and an agreement was reached: the Soviets took the missiles out of Cuba, and we made a big show out of taking some missiles out of Turkey, a country near Russia.

Eventually, many years later, for lots of reasons—including a lack of blue jeans and rock and roll and not enough bread on peoples' tables—the Soviet government fell, and people said the Cold War was over.

That house with the escape map on the wall was sold a couple of years after the missile crisis ended, and my sister wasn't born in a bomb shelter after all.

But most of those nuclear weapons are still around—and more and more countries still seem to want nuclear weapons of their own, thinking such weapons will make them tougher and keep their leaders in power longer.

And not just countries: political and religious groups with an ax to grind want those weapons, too. It's that strange grown-up behavior again: being willing to destroy things to prove how much better you are than someone else.

I'm a grown-up now myself, and a dad. I keep an eye on my sons' walls to see if they ever feel the need to draw escape maps of their own.

We all hope that the grown-ups can stay smart enough to keep from blowing things up.

THE PRESIDENTIAL PET

written and illustrated by
STEVEN KELLOGG

Every four years after a national election, it is inevitable that the losing party will gloomily assert that "the White House has gone to the dogs." In truth, however, the nation's most celebrated residence has always been a kennel no matter which party was in power. Very few of our chief executives have dared to face the relentless stress of a term in office without the companionship, support, and solace that are unconditionally available from a devoted dog. Despite revelations of appalling presidential ineptitude, or humiliating misbehavior, or pitiable poll standings, the dog will never vote to impeach his master. He is the only constituent whose affection and loyalty are immune to disillusionment, and thus the unofficial cabinet post of First Pet is crucially important to the security of any head of state. More than a few cats have served with distinction, and occasionally a representative of a less traditional species has occupied the post.

What would happen if a collection of presidential pets were to suddenly assemble on the White House lawn? Imagine them arriving in the company of the chief executives with whom they once shared relaxing strolls, intimate snuggles, exhilarating romps, or the challenges and triumphs of an intense housebreaking campaign.

As the former commanders in chief emerge from the shadows of the past, the shock of mutual recognition would instantly awaken their contentious political natures. Presidential hackles would rise, and the hunger for preeminence that once drove them to compete for the highest office in the land would now compel them to organize a Presidential Pet Show!

Each one of them would imagine himself proudly leading his beloved companion into the winner's circle while pretending not to notice the expressions of dismay on the faces of his rejected colleagues. Each one of them would imagine savoring the heady feeling of having his superiority confirmed as he accepts the Best in Show trophy.

Please turn the page and follow the father of our country and his pack of hounds into the ring, where you will meet the assembled contestants.

GEORGE WASHINGTON and his hounds
Sweet Lips, Tipsy, Tipler, Cloe, Searcher, Taster, and Drunkard

My Room

LYNDA JOHNSON ROBB

ILLUSTRATED BY JANE DYER

I WAS A SOPHOMORE IN COLLEGE living away from home in a dorm at the University of Texas. Then, suddenly, everything changed. After the assassination in November 1963, my parents decided that if I lived with them, I would not only be safer, but I would also be of help to them. So I came to Washington, D.C., to live in the White House.

I envisioned the family quarters at the White House decorated with antiques, every piece with a fascinating historical provenance. When I arrived in my room, previously occupied by Caroline Kennedy, I found no antiques, only the same furniture that had been in my old bedroom. There were antiques in the official rooms on the first floor, but the family quarters were furnished with a mix of furniture that Mother had found at the government warehouse and pieces she had brought from our previous homes. I had imagined that I would be sleeping if not in a bed christened by Abigail Adams herself, our first White House First Lady, at least in one that Andrew Jackson or one of the Teddy Roosevelt children had used. Instead, it was just like home, only with a more exciting view.

My room on the second floor faced the entrance on Pennsylvania Avenue and overlooked the large lantern above the main White House entrance. Here heads of state would arrive for state dinners. Although official dinners didn't happen often, five days a week tourists finished their tours by going out that same door and down the driveway back to Pennsylvania Avenue. In our day, the White House was open for special tours early in the mornings and then on a first-come, first-served basis from ten to noon. After walking through the rooms on the ground floor and ceremonial first floor, the sightseers would exit right under my window. What a noise they would make! Some days when I was trying to sleep late or when I was studying, I felt like opening the window and dropping a water balloon on them. Wisely, I never did.

I imagined that hundreds of famous people had shared that room with me through the ages. As a history student, I decided I would try to discover the facts about the room's historical life. I visited the White House curator, who couldn't recall any famous people who had shared that room. I interviewed President Eisenhower when he came for a visit. He remembered only that Queen Elizabeth's lady-in-waiting had stayed there. I was finding out that not only had George Washington not slept there, no one famous had. Finally I gave up on my search.

After that, all the discoveries I made about my room came by accident. In a movie, I heard that "after little Willie Lincoln died, they locked up his room, never to go in it."

"What room was that?" I asked the White House curator.

"That was your room, Lynda," he answered.

Then I read a book that revealed that after President Lincoln was shot, his body was brought back to the White House, where the autopsy was performed. It described a long hallway leading to the room where it took place: yes, it was my room. The bad news didn't stop there, for death seemed to follow my room. I soon learned that only a short time before I moved in, President Truman's mother-in-law had died in "my" room. That was the last straw. My curiosity had uncovered information that was better left swept under the rug, no matter who had stood on it before.

White House Souvenir

short story by **Polly Horvath**

illustrated by **Sophie Blackall**

"**YOU CAN'T TAKE ANYTHING**," I cautioned my sister as we headed over for our White House tour. "Finding" souvenirs had always been Marsha's favorite part of taking trips. "People are watching."

"So they claim. If you're willing to believe everything *they* tell you. Anyhow, people have made off with a load of stuff in the past, and why not? It's as much your house as theirs. Listen, my taxes paid for the toilet paper in there."

"You can't take that either, because the closest restroom for visitors is in the Ellipse Visitor Pavilion."

"I've got something more original planned than toilet paper," said Marsha scathingly. I shuddered.

"You can't take anything, really," I went on worriedly. "No backpacks, handbags, personal grooming devices—basically nothing at all is allowed inside. No scissors, knives, or knitting needles."

"Have they had problems with people settling in to knit? Never mind. The scissors, I admit, are a loss. I'd say a good fifty percent of souvenirs taken in the past required scissors.

Snippets of carpet were taken, tassels from the curtains cut off and pocketed, presumably when the staff was looking the other way. Then again, who knows, maybe it was encouraged, because it deflected attention from the babies' and dogs' hair. People love taking hair. You know that your fellow citizens chopped off bits of Franklin Roosevelt's dog Fala's fur and of baby Ruth Cleveland's tresses?"

"Oh, come on," I protested.

"I assure you. Andrew Jackson was apparently so used to people sneaking up behind him with nail scissors that he cut off and passed out his own souvenir locks. Zachary Taylor's warhorse, Old Whitey, lost most of his tail that way. And it wasn't just hair. The curtains got cut to shreds. Yep, scissors are a loss to the souvenir hunter's art."

By this time I was in a dead sweat. The metal detectors were up ahead. But we glided through.

"The inside of the White House is impressive, all right," said Marsha, peering around corners. "You can't exactly see someone putting his feet up and eating Doritos in it, but I'm sure the First Family's quarters, which we don't get to see, are comfortable in a kind of hello–good-bye way. I don't think you can really cozy up to any place you know you're just passing through."

"Actually, I'm amazed there's anything left in the way of furnishings," I said.

"Well, you have to leave them something. Say, look at that marvelous light fixture! Now, wouldn't I like to get up there. Nobler women than I have taken crystal pendants from the chandeliers. They took spoons, too. Of course, anyone can take a spoon. Franklin Roosevelt's housekeeper stopped using spoons at White House teas because they all disappeared. Can you imagine going to a White House tea and having to stir with your fingers?"

"I'm certain nobody stirred with their fingers," I said.

"Probably," said Marsha. "One president, I think it was William Taft, trained the Secret Service to help out at dinners just to put the brakes on some of the nightly loss of bric-a-brac. Can you imagine, you've spent years learning how to deal with national security, you're a crack shot, and your job for the night is to go around saying, 'Let me help you put that fork back'? Well, it's too tawdry if you ask me."

"Exactly," I said warningly.

"Oh, don't be such a worrywart," said Marsha as she bent down to tie her shoe.

Once we were out in the fresh air again, I breathed a sigh of relief. "I'm so glad you didn't take anything."

"I don't know why you're making such a big deal out if it," sniffed Marsha. "Even the presidents' families took stuff. President Johnson nabbed the Air Force One china for his ranch in Texas, and Maureen Reagan made off with about a million matchbooks."

"Oh, well, matchbooks . . ." I said. "I suspect everyone at state dinners takes those."

"That's right, because *souvenir* means remembrance, and this is the People's House, and they like to remember it the way any red-blooded American would—with *stuff*. I think it's a sign of love for your country to scale the curtains and hang from the chandeliers just to nab a little bit of history. But I knew you'd object. So I figured that if you can take something from the White House, you can leave something too. When I knelt down to tie my shoe, I left a little lock of my own hair on the White House floor. Now the White House has a souvenir of *me*."

There was a long silence as I digested this.

"You know they vacuum, Marsha, don't you?" I said finally.

"So they claim," said Marsha. "So they claim."

Robert F. Kennedy's Remarks on the Assassination of Martin Luther King, Jr.

April 4, 1968

Ladies and gentlemen,

I'm only going to talk to you just for a minute or so this evening, because I have some—some very sad news for all of you, . . . and, I think, sad news for all of our fellow citizens, and people who love peace all over the world; and that is that Martin Luther King was shot and was killed tonight in Memphis, Tennessee.

Martin Luther King dedicated his life to love and to justice between fellow human beings. He died in the cause of that effort. In this difficult day, in this difficult time for the United States, it's perhaps well to ask what kind of a nation we are and what direction we want to move in. For those of you who are black—considering the evidence evidently is that there were white people who were responsible—you can be filled with bitterness, and with hatred, and a desire for revenge.

We can move in that direction as a country, in greater polarization—black people amongst blacks, and white amongst whites, filled with hatred toward one another. Or we can make an effort, as Martin Luther King did, to understand, and to comprehend, and replace that violence, that stain of bloodshed that has spread across our land, with an effort to understand, compassion, and love.

For those of you who are black and are tempted to fill with—be filled with hatred and mistrust of the injustice of such an act, against all white people, I would only say that I can also feel in my own heart the same kind of feeling. I had a member of my family killed, but he was killed by a white man.

But we have to make an effort in the United States. We have to make an effort to understand, to get beyond, or go beyond these rather difficult times.

My favorite poem, my—my favorite poet was Aeschylus. And he once wrote:

Even in our sleep, pain which cannot forget
falls drop by drop upon the heart,
until, in our own despair,
against our will,
comes wisdom
through the awful grace of God.

What we need in the United States is not division; what we need in the United States is not hatred; what we need in the United States is not violence and lawlessness, but is love, and wisdom, and compassion toward one another, and a feeling of justice toward those who still suffer within our country, whether they be white or whether they be black.

So I ask you tonight to return home, to say a prayer for the family of Martin Luther King—yeah, it's true—but more importantly to say a prayer for our own country, which all of us love—a prayer for understanding and that compassion of which I spoke.

We can do well in this country. We will have difficult times. We've had difficult times in the past, but we—and we will have difficult times in the future. It is not the end of violence; it is not the end of lawlessness; and it's not the end of disorder.

But the vast majority of white people and the vast majority of black people in this country want to live together, want to improve the quality of our life, and want justice for all human beings that abide in our land.

And let's dedicate ourselves to what the Greeks wrote so many years ago: to tame the savageness of man and make gentle the life of this world. Let us dedicate ourselves to that, and say a prayer for our country and for our people.

Thank you very much.

Black White House / White Black House
ILLUSTRATION BY
Chris Raschka

PRESIDENT RICHARD M. NIXON'S FINAL REMARKS TO THE WHITE HOUSE STAFF

August 9, 1974

MEMBERS OF THE CABINET, members of the White House staff, all of our friends here:

. . .You are here to say good-bye to us, and we don't have a good word for it in English—the best is *au revoir*. ("We'll see you again.")

I just met with the members of the White House staff, you know, those that serve here in the White House day in and day out, and I asked them to do what I ask all of you to do to the extent that you can and, of course, are requested to do so: to serve our next president as you have served me and previous presidents—because many of you have been here for many years with devotion and dedication—because this office, great as it is, can only be as great as the men and women who work for and with the president.

This house, for example—I was thinking of it as we walked down this hall, and I was comparing it to some of the great houses of the world that I've been in. This isn't the biggest house. Many, and most, in even smaller countries, are much bigger. This isn't the finest house. Many in Europe, particularly, and in China, Asia, have paintings of great, great value, things that we just don't have here, and probably will never have until we are one thousand years old or older.

But this is the best house. It's the best house because it has something far more important than numbers of people who serve, far more important than numbers of rooms or how big it is, far more important than numbers of magnificent pieces of art.

This house has a great heart, and that heart comes from those who serve. . . .

And so I say to you on this occasion as we leave, we leave proud of the people who have stood by us and worked for us and served this country. We want you to be proud of what you've done. We want you to continue to serve in government, if that is your wish. Always give your best; never get discouraged; never be petty. Always remember, others may hate you, but those who hate you don't win unless you hate them, and then you destroy yourself.

And so, we leave with high hopes, in good spirit and with deep humility, and with very much gratefulness in our hearts. I can only say to each and every one of you, we come from many faiths, we pray perhaps to different gods, but really the same God in a sense, but I want to say for each and every one of you, not only will we always remember you, not only will we always be grateful to you, but always you will be in our hearts and you will be in our prayers.

Thank you very much.

THE WHITE HOUSE
WASHINGTON

August 9, 1974

Dear Mr. Secretary:

I hereby resign the Office of President of the United States.

Sincerely,

Richard Nixon

The Honorable Henry A. Kissinger
The Secretary of State
Washington, D. C. 20520

11.35 AM

HK

ILLUSTRATION BY
ROXIE MUNRO

PART VII

THE GREAT HOUSE
ENDURES

From *Christmas in Plains: Memories*

Jimmy Carter

illustrated by Don Powers

·1979·

As CHRISTMAS APPROACHED in 1979, both our nation and I were obsessed with the plight of American hostages who had been captured when Iranian militants took over our embassy in Teheran during the first week in November. It seemed especially sad that such an act of international terrorism would be continuing during this holy season of peace and goodwill. . . .

Although we had decided to restrict our personal travels, Rosalynn and I felt that we should have the regular holiday observances at the White House. We realized how much pleasure our visitors got from such social affairs, and we didn't want to let the Iranian terrorists have the satisfaction of interfering in these precious events. For many afternoons and nights during the holiday season, we followed the tradition of America's First Families by holding a constant series of receptions.

Among many others, we entertained members of the Secret Service and the executive police around the White House, with all their families—about a thousand people. We had the directors of the intelligence community, Office of Management and Budget, General Services Administration, Federal Emergency Management Agency, Cabinet members, our own staff members, and the White House press corps. . . .

One of the most emotional events that Christmas season came when we had the annual lighting of the national tree on the Ellipse. Amy and I planned a big surprise for the ceremony. When the television cameras focused on her at the crucial moment, she threw the switch but no lights lit up on the tree except the single Star of Hope on top—a symbolic acknowledgment that we were not celebrating while our hostages were being held, but were confident that all of them would return safely and to freedom. We had placed a row of small trees around the park, one for each hostage, with blue lights on them. Afterward, I received more favorable comments about the surprise lighting than about almost anything else I've ever done. I had thought this was the first event of its kind, but someone told me that the national tree was not lighted for three years during World War II. . . .

. . . I realized that it was going to be a lonely Christmas. Our last-minute decision to stay at Camp David had caught our sons and their families by surprise, and they were spending the holidays in Plains or with in-laws, so Rosalynn, Amy, and I were to be the only family members there.

More than any others in our family, Amy was immersed in the lives of the White House staff, spending hours in the kitchen and other places with the cooks, stewards, laundry workers, ushers, maids, butlers, and maintenance men. When I mentioned how empty Camp David seemed, she replied that very few of these loyal workers had ever been to Camp David, although many of them had served in the White House for several decades and some were approaching retirement. We agreed with her suggestion to invite all of them to come up and spend Christmas Day with us, with no responsibilities at all except that the Filipino stewards already on duty would prepare a festive meal for everybody.

We three exchanged personal gifts in our cabin quite early Christmas morning, read the Christmas story once again, and then, at daylight, we began calling our families in Plains and talked to everyone we could get on the phone. Afterward, we spent several hours with two busloads of our friends from the White House, who brought their families with them. We enjoyed acting as guides, showing off the various cabins, the swimming pool, the bowling alley, the room where we had Sunday religious services, and answering

their questions about how the Egyptians and Israelis had lived and worked during the long peace talks. After a Christmas dinner of turkey with all the trimmings and individual photographs with each family, we waved goodbye to the buses. Their visit had turned our potentially lonely Christmas Day into one that we would never forget.

At the same time, I couldn't forget about the American hostages being held in Teheran, and was wondering what else I might do to hasten their release. . . .

·1980·

Twelve months later, in 1980, we approached Christmas with few reasons for celebration. I had lost the election and would soon be out of office. Fifty-two hostages were still being held in Iran, but we were encouraged by reports from the Algerians that the Ayatollah Khomeini was contemplating their release during the holiday season. . . .

My last hours in office were filled with high drama. I never went to bed Sunday or Monday night, and we finally realized that our intense negotiations had been successful when Tuesday morning dawned—inauguration day.

The Iranians yielded on all the major points of our discussions, agreeing to our holding $12 billion to resolve financial claims, and to the safe release of all the American captives. Two hours before my term was to end, I was informed that all of them were in a plane at the end of the runway in Teheran, poised to take off for Wiesbaden, Germany, where they would be given physical examinations and where I would later meet them. The plane was in the air with all the hostages on board while my successor was making his acceptance speech. We celebrated all the way to Georgia, my last ride in Air Force One.

THE WHITE HOUSE

JON SCIESZKA

ILLUSTRATED BY TONY FUCILE

White House, O White House, place of great fame,

Don't you think it's a bit of a shame

That for this grand residence,

Home of our presidents,

That's the best we could do for a name?

RONALD REAGAN
PHOTOGRAPH BY
DIANA WALKER

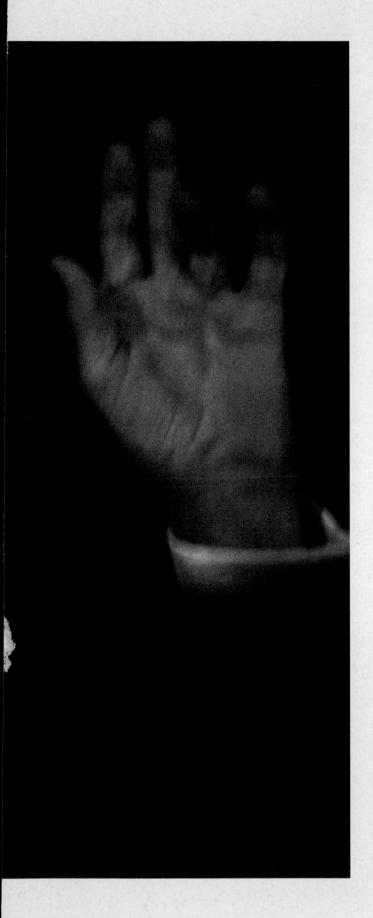

From Ronald Reagan's Farewell Address to the Nation, January 11, 1989

You know, down the hall and up the stairs from this office is the part of the White House where the president and his family live. There are a few favorite windows I have up there that I like to stand and look out of early in the morning. The view is over the grounds here to the Washington Monument, and then the Mall and the Jefferson Memorial. But on mornings when the humidity is low, you can see past the Jefferson to the river, the Potomac, and the Virginia shore. Someone said that's the view Lincoln had when he saw the smoke rising from the Battle of Bull Run. I see more prosaic things: the grass on the banks, the morning traffic as people make their way to work, now and then a sailboat on the river. . . .

. . . The past few days when I've been at that window upstairs, I've thought a bit of the "shining city upon a hill." The phrase comes from John Winthrop, who wrote it to describe the America he imagined. What he imagined was important because he was an early Pilgrim, an early freedom man. He journeyed here on what today we'd call a little wooden boat; and like the other Pilgrims, he was looking for a home that would be free.

I've spoken of the shining city all my political life, but I don't know if I ever quite communicated what I saw when I said it. But in my mind it was a tall, proud city built on rocks stronger than oceans, windswept, God-blessed, and teeming with people of all kinds living in harmony and peace; a city with free ports that hummed with commerce and creativity. And if there had to be city walls, the walls had doors and the doors were open to anyone with the will and the heart to get here. That's how I saw it, and see it still.

December 31, 1990
Dear George, Jeb, Neil, Marvin, Doro,

I am writing this letter on the last day of 1990.

First, I can't begin to tell you how great it was to have you here at Camp David. I loved the games (the Marines are still smarting over their 1 and 2 record*), I loved Christmas Day, marred only by the absence of Sam and Ellie.† I loved the movies—some of 'em—I loved the laughs. Most of all, I loved seeing you together. We are a family blessed, and this Christmas simply reinforced all that.

I hope I didn't seem moody. I tried not to.

When I came into this job, I vowed I would never wring my hands and talk about "the loneliest job in the world" or wring my hands about the "pressures or the trials."

Having said that, I have been concerned about what lies ahead. There is no "loneliness," though, because I am backed by a first-rate team of knowledgeable and committed people. No president has been more blessed in this regard.

I have thought long and hard about what might have to be done. As I write this letter at year's end, there is still some hope that Iraq's dictator will pull out of Kuwait. I vary on this. Sometimes I think he might, at others I think he simply is too unrealistic—too ignorant of what he might face. I have the peace of mind that comes from knowing that we have tried hard for peace. We have gone to the UN; we have formed an historic coalition; there have been diplomatic initiatives from country after country.

And so here we are a scant 16 days from a very important date—the date set by the UN for his total compliance with all UN resolutions, including getting out of Kuwait—totally.

I guess what I want you to know as a father is this: Every human life is precious. When the question is asked "How many lives are you willing to sacrifice?"—it tears at my heart. The answer, of course, is none—none at all.

GEORGE H. W. BUSH
PHOTOGRAPH BY
DIANA WALKER

GEORGE H. W. AND BARBARA BUSH
PHOTOGRAPH BY
DIANA WALKER

DIANA WALKER/TIME

We have waited to give sanctions a chance; we have moved a tremendous force so as to reduce the risk to every American soldier if force has to be used; but the question of loss of life still lingers and plagues my heart.

My mind goes back to history:

How many lives might have been saved if appeasement had given way to force earlier on in the late '30s or earliest '40s? How many Jews might have been spared the gas chambers, or how many Polish patriots might be alive today? I look at today's crisis as "good" vs. "evil"—Yes, it is that clear.

I know my stance must cause you a little grief from time to time and this hurts me; but here at "year's end" I just wanted you to know that I feel:

—every human life is precious—the little Iraqi kids' too.

—principle must be adhered to—Saddam cannot profit in any way at all from his aggression and from his brutalizing the people of Kuwait.

—and sometimes in life you have to act as you think best—you can't compromise, you can't give in—even if your critics are loud and numerous.

So, dear kids—batten down the hatches.

Senator Inouye of Hawaii told me, "Mr. President, do what you have to do. If it is quick and successful everyone can take the credit. If it is drawn out, then be prepared for some in Congress to file impeachment papers against you"—That's what he said, and he's 100% correct.

And so I shall say a few more prayers, mainly for our kids in the Gulf. And I shall do what must be done, and I shall be strengthened every day by our family love, which lifts me up, every single day of my life.

I am the luckiest dad in the whole wide world.

I love you, Happy New Year, and may God bless every one of you and all those in your family.

> *Devotedly,*
>
> *Dad*

---

* In wallyball, which is volleyball played in a racquetball court, the walls are "in play."

† They had spent Christmas with their father. Doro and Billy had divorced earlier in the year.

The Secret Service

dialogue imagined by Jess M. Brallier
illustrated by David Small

Ever wonder who all those guys are that you see in the movies and on the news whenever you see the president? You know who I mean . . . the men and women who all wear dark clothes and sunglasses and have little wires hanging from their ears. They're Secret Service agents, working at the White House and on the road to protect the president and others.

Secret Service: **So, you'd like to join the Secret Service?**

You: Sure. I love the president. Protecting him sounds like a great job. What an honor.

SS: **Are you prepared to risk your personal safety for him?**

You: Hmm. Get hurt? Sure. I could handle an injured leg or something . . . a shoulder, maybe.

SS: **You might even have to risk your life.**

You: Wow. OK. Let's say I'd do anything to protect the president. Then do I get to live at the White House with him?

SS: **Sorry; that's classified. Our agents are constantly on duty at the White House, but we can't talk about exactly how many there are or what your living arrangements might be until you pass all the tests. Now, do you understand that the Secret Service does much more than just protect the president?**

You: Really? Like what?

SS: **Well, the Secret Service was founded in 1865 to combat counterfeit money production in the United States. Today we still investigate counterfeit money, as well as credit card, computer, and financial institution fraud.**

You: Financial institution fraud? That sounds complicated. I'm not that good at math.

SS: We do a lot of statistics and such, so you have to be good at basic math as well as fractions, decimals, and averages if you want to join the Service.

You: Part of the reason I want to join the Secret Service is that they're always using those cool-looking dogs. I really like those dogs.

SS: Those dogs may look cute, but they're serious about their job. They're called Belgian Malinois. They were originally bred in Belgium, but ours are from Holland. They have extra-short hair that helps them focus on their work, even in the heat.

You: Hmm. Maybe I could train them. I'll teach them all sorts of fun tricks, like rolling over, playing dead, and go fetch.

SS: Those dogs train for twenty straight weeks to become members of the Service. Then, every week until they retire, they train for another eight hours to stay on the ball.

You: That's a well-trained dog! What about protecting someone besides the president? Maybe someone not so much in the spotlight? You guys do that?

SS: Sure. We're in charge of protecting the president, the vice president, former presidents, the president's family, and other important members of our government and visitors representing foreign governments.

You: Yeah, that sounds more up my alley. I'll protect one of those guys. When can I start?

SS: First you need a college degree.

You: Can do.

SS: Besides that, you need to be in good shape and not have a criminal record.

You: No problem.

SS: After that, you come down to Georgia and spend nine weeks in a training center, learning the skills police use.

You: I'm going to be busy.

SS: And after that, you have to undergo another twelve weeks of special Secret Service training in Washington, D.C. If you make it through all of that, then it's welcome to the Secret Service.

You: I'll get back to you.

I LIVE IN THE WHITE HOUSE

JACK PRELUTSKY ILLUSTRATED BY JIM LaMARCHE

I live in the White House
and do as I please.
Nobody stops me
or asks for IDs.
Nobody minds
that I wander the halls;
I don't always come
when the President calls.

I live in the White House,
and not as a guest;
I don't have to work,
and I never get dressed.
I'm often around
when the Cabinet's there
and crouch in a corner—
they don't seem to care.

I've plenty to drink,
and I've plenty to eat.
I even take naps
at the President's feet.
Because I'm his pet,
I'm completely at ease.
I live in the White House
and do as I please.

From *Meet the Press with Tim Russert:* Interview with Vice President Dick Cheney, September 16, 2001

MR. TIM RUSSERT: And we are at Greentop, in the shadows of the presidential retreat at Camp David. Mr. Vice President, good morning and welcome.

VICE PRESIDENT DICK CHENEY: Good morning, Tim.

MR. RUSSERT: Let me turn to the events of Tuesday. Where were you when you first learned a plane had struck the World Trade Center?

VICE PRESIDENT CHENEY: Well, I was in my office Tuesday morning. Monday, I had been in Kentucky, and the president had been in the White House. Tuesday, our roles were sort of reversed. He was in Florida, and I was in the White House Tuesday morning. And a little before nine, my speechwriter came in. We were going to go over some speeches coming up. And my secretary called in just as we were starting to meet, just before nine o'clock, and said an airplane had hit the World Trade Center, and that was the first one that went in. So we turned on the television and watched for a few minutes and then actually saw the second plane hit the World Trade Center. And the—as soon as that second plane showed up, that's what triggered the thought: terrorism, that this was an attack.

MR. RUSSERT: You sensed it immediately, "This is deliberate"?

VICE PRESIDENT CHENEY: Yeah. Then I convened in my office. Condi Rice came down. Her office is right near mine there in the West Wing.

MR. RUSSERT: The national security adviser.

VICE PRESIDENT CHENEY: National security adviser, my chief of staff, Scooter Libby, Mary Matalin, who works for me, convened in my office, and we started talking about getting the Counterterrorism Task Force up and operating. I talked with the president. I'd given word to Andy Card's staff, who is right next door, to get hold of Andy and/or the president and that I wanted to talk to him as soon as they could hook it up. This call came in, and the president knew at this point about that. We discussed a statement that he might make, and the first statement he made describing this as an act of apparent terrorism flowed out of those conversations. While I was there, over the next several minutes, watching developments on the television and as we started to get organized to figure out what to do, my Secret Service agents came in and, under these circumstances, they just move. They don't say "sir" or ask politely. They came in and said, "Sir, we have to leave immediately," and grabbed me and . . .

MR. RUSSERT: Literally grabbed you and moved you?

VICE PRESIDENT CHENEY: Yeah. And, you know, your feet touch the floor periodically. But they're bigger than I am, and they hoisted me up and moved me very rapidly down the hallway, down some stairs, through some doors, and down some more stairs into an underground facility under the White House, and, as a matter of fact, it's a corridor, locked at both ends, and they did that because they had received a report that an airplane was headed for the White House.

MR. RUSSERT: This is Flight 77, which had left Dulles.

VICE PRESIDENT CHENEY: Which turned out to be Flight 77. It left Dulles, flown west towards Ohio, been captured by the terrorists. They turned off the transponder, which led to a later report that a plane had gone down in Ohio, but it really hadn't. Of course, then they turned back and headed back towards Washington. As best we can tell, they came initially at the White House and . . .

MR. RUSSERT: The plane actually circled the White House?

VICE PRESIDENT CHENEY: Didn't circle it, but was headed on a track into it. The Secret Service has an arrangement with the FAA. They had open lines after the World Trade Center was . . .

MR. RUSSERT: Tracking it by radar.

VICE PRESIDENT CHENEY: And when it entered the danger zone and looked like it was headed for the White House was when they grabbed me and evacuated me to the basement. The plane obviously didn't hit the White House. It turned away and, we think, flew a circle and came back in and then hit the Pentagon. And that's what the radar track looks like. The result of that—once I got down into the shelter, the first thing I did—there's a secure phone there. First thing I did was pick up the telephone and call the president again, who was still down in Florida, at that point, and strongly urged him to delay his return.

MR. RUSSERT: You told him to stay away from Washington.

VICE PRESIDENT CHENEY: I said, "Delay your return. We don't know what's going on here, but it looks like, you know, we've been targeted."

From *THE 9/11 COMMISSION REPORT*

AT THE WHITE HOUSE, Vice President Dick Cheney had just sat down for a meeting when his assistant told him to turn on his television because a plane had struck the North Tower of the World Trade Center. The Vice President was wondering "how … could a plane hit the World Trade Center" when he saw the second aircraft strike the South Tower. . . .

The President was seated in a classroom when, at 9:05, Andrew Card whispered to him: "A second plane hit the second tower. America is under attack." . . .

The President remained in the classroom for another five to seven minutes. . . . He then returned to a holding room shortly before 9:15, where he was briefed by staff and saw television coverage. He next spoke to Vice President Cheney, Dr. Rice, New York Governor George Pataki, and FBI Director Robert Mueller. He decided to make a brief statement from the school before leaving for the airport. The Secret Service told us they were anxious to move the President to a safer location, but did not think it imperative for him to run out the door. . . .

The President's motorcade departed at 9:35, and arrived at the airport between 9:42 and 9:45. During the ride the President learned about the attack on the Pentagon. He boarded the aircraft, asked the Secret Service about the safety of his family, and called the Vice President. . . .The President told the Vice President: "Sounds like we have a minor war going on here, I heard about the Pentagon. We're at war. . . somebody's going to pay." . . .

American 77 began turning south, away from the White House, at 9:34. It continued heading south for roughly a minute, before turning west and beginning to circle back. This news prompted the Secret Service to order the immediate evacuation of the Vice President just before 9:36. Agents propelled him out of his chair and told him he had to get to the bunker. The Vice President entered the underground tunnel leading to the shelter at 9:37. . . .

. . .The Vice President asked to speak to the President, but it took time for the call to be connected. He learned in the tunnel that the Pentagon had been hit. . . .

. . . At 9:55 the Vice President was still on the phone with the President. . . . We believe this is the same call in which the Vice President urged the President not to return to Washington. . . .

. . . There is conflicting evidence about when the Vice President arrived in the shelter conference room. . . . The Vice President recalled being told, just after his arrival, that the Air Force was trying to establish a combat air patrol [CAP] over Washington.

The Vice President stated that he called the President to discuss the rules of engagement for the CAP. He recalled feeling that it did no good to establish the CAP unless the pilots had instructions on whether they were authorized to shoot if the plane would not divert. He said the President signed off on that concept. The President said he remembered such a conversation, and that it reminded him of when he had been an interceptor pilot. The President emphasized to us that he had authorized the shootdown of hijacked aircraft. . . .

Among the sources that reflect other important events of that morning, there is no documentary evidence for this call, but the relevant sources are incomplete. . . .

At some time between 10:10 and 10:15, a military aide told the Vice President and others that the aircraft was 80 miles out. Vice President Cheney was asked for authority to engage the aircraft. His reaction was described by Scooter Libby as quick and decisive, "in about the time it takes a batter to decide to swing." The Vice President authorized fighter aircraft to engage the inbound plane. He told us he based this authorization on his earlier conversation with the President. The military aide returned a few minutes later, probably between 10:12 and 10:18, and said the aircraft was 60 miles out. He again asked for authorization to engage. The Vice President again said yes.

At the conference room table was White House Deputy Chief of Staff Joshua Bolten. Bolten watched the exchanges and, after what he called "a quiet moment," suggested that the Vice President get in touch with the President and confirm the engage order. Bolten told us he wanted to make sure the President was told that the Vice President had executed the order. He said he had not heard any prior discussion on the subject with the President.

The Vice President was logged calling the President at 10:18 for a two-minute conversation that obtained the confirmation. On Air Force One, the President's press secretary was taking notes; Ari Fleischer recorded that at 10:20, the President told him that he had authorized a shootdown of aircraft if necessary.

Visiting the White House

Sarah Stewart

From my diary — 23 May '04

Riding from Dulles Airport to Washington, D.C., the power center of the United States, we could be approaching any large metropolitan area in the East. The highway is an endless thruway of green directional signs, bland hotels, and noisy, numbing traffic. But as we enter the city and the White House comes into view, a wave of goose bumps surges across my skin. The White House is unique, and it belongs to us.

Our taxi driver was born in Saudi Arabia "thirty years ago next week—but I'm an American citizen now." The young woman who greets us at the hotel's reception desk is from South Africa. "I've been an American citizen for almost a year," she announces. Our waiter at lunch, originally from El Salvador, is also now a citizen. We linger in the restaurant, looking at our map, and a different man comes over to fill our coffee cups. He's from Vietnam and is "very proud" to be an American citizen. The concierge, who tells us how to walk to the White House visitors' gate, is Iranian, and the man who brings our bags to our room is Sudanese. Both are citizens now. We are all Americans, and the White House belongs to all of us.

Backstairs at the White House
A More or Less ON-THE-SPOT Sketch Journal
David Small

THE GREEN HOUSE

imagined by MEGAN McDONALD

From the desk of Mrs. Binkley

To the President of the United States:

Enclosed please find letters from some of the nation's most concerned citizens, my fourth-graders at Rachel Carson Elementary. We are doing a unit on the environment, and my students thought of ways to help save the globe. I hope you will find them as honest, funny, and wise as I did.

Sincerely,
Mrs. Binkley

Dear Mr. President,

I have a funny joke for you. How many presidents does it take to change a lightbulb?

The answer is one.

Because all you have to do is stand on a chair (unless you are super-duper tall, like Abe Lincoln) and change one regular bulb to one of those fancy new ones that look like soft-serve ice-cream cones (yum!). Mrs. Binkley told us that if every person in the U.S. replaced ONE lightbulb with the ice-cream-cone kind, the energy saved could light 2.5 million homes for one whole entire year!!!

That is a fact, Mr. President. Also a fact is that it would be like taking almost a million cars off the road, and you have to believe me, since our class learned this from the Department of Energy and I heard you are their boss.

Your ice-cream buddy,
Maddie Hanson

Dear Mr. President:

My idea for how the White House can help save energy and help save the earth is that you should change the name of the White House to the Green House. I hope you like my idea. The end.

Signed,
Olivia Martinez

Dear Mr. President,

We are learning about the environment and how to help save the earth. Our class has so many ideas that we started a club called the Green Beanies. (I voted for it to be called the Green Meanies, but we're not supposed to be mean, just nice.)

So don't be a Green Weenie! Go green!

I can't tell you what to do, since you are, after all, the president, but I know you have a lot of grass to cut on your big lawn where you hunt Easter eggs. So instead of using mowers that are loud and burn gas and oil and pollute, you could get some goats or a sheep to eat the grass. Because in our fourth-grade social studies book, we saw a picture of President William Howard Taft's cow, Pauline, outside the White House, and that is what gave me the great idea. Also we learned that President Woodpile Wilson had a flock of sheep to eat all the grass back during World War I. And President Benjamin Somebody had a goat named His Whiskers.

W.B.S. (Write Back Soon.)

Your friend,

Jennifer Wayland

P.S. If you get a sheep, could you name her Jennifer?

Mr. President,

Be a vampire slayer!

We heard in our class that you have vampires at the White House.

Ha, ha. But this kind you can't chase away with stinky garlic.

Vampires, in case you did not know, are sneaky things that take up energy when you're not even there, like a computer you're not using. If we all shut off our electric stuff when we aren't using it, we could save billions!

Now you know why I wrote this by hand without a computer (on recycled paper).

Yours truly,

Matthew Whaley

Dear Mr. President:

I have an idea, and here it is. I think that you should carpool with that Air Force One plane of yours. Because all I ever see is you and the Number One Lady getting off the plane and waving. (Hi, by the way!)

But guess what? I think some other people would like to ride on that plane too. Is the vice president your best friend? He will be if you let him ride on your plane with you. A plane puts tons of greenhouse gases in the air, and I am really, really, really, really, really worried about the polar bears. Penguins, too.

Your friend Zack

Mr. President:

In our class we learned about the sun and solar energy. A lot of us in Mrs. Binkley's class (the Green Beanies) think that the White House should put solar panels on the roof. This could help heat up water and stuff. Our teacher told us President Jimmy Carter really did put solar panels on the roof back in the 1970s. But now they are in a museum. What are they doing there?

Maybe you should call up Mr. President Jimmy Carter and talk to him about those solar panels.

BRING BACK SOLAR ENERGY!!!!!!!

Sarah Jameson

Dear Mr. President:

I hear you have a ghost in the White House, up in Lincoln's old bedroom. It must be pretty drafty in that room for a ghost to slip through the cracks. I think if you plug up all the cracks you'll save 30 percent more energy, keep the heat in, and — you guessed it — keep the ghosts out, too!

Ghostbuster Nick Vespa

Dear Mr. President:

If the White House has 35 bathrooms and every person uses 50 pounds of toilet paper per year, multiply 35 X 50 (we learned double digits this year) and you are using at least 1,750 pounds of t.p. over there in your big house.

You must know a lot of smart people, and I think somebody could invent the Three-Square Toilet-Paper Wizard. This cuts down on waste because only three squares of t.p. come out at one time, and this will save a LOT of trees. Don't forget you can make stuff out of the empty cardboard tubes, too, like (1) hamster toys, (2) puppets, (3) kazoos, (4) snakes, and (5) candy holders.

Your "pal"indrome,
Noah Haon

P.S. If you want to use any of my ideas, please send $7.50 to this address: 1111 School Lane, Gatorsburg, MD.

The First Pitch

Stephanie True Peters

illustrated by Matt Tavares

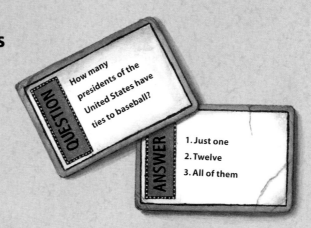

From George Washington to George W. Bush, every United States president has been associated with baseball in some way. At Valley Forge, Washington played a game called rounders, the predecessor to today's game. "He sometimes throws and catches a ball for hours with his aide-de-camp," a soldier serving under the general noted in a letter.

When Abraham Lincoln was president, he often joined children to play a game similar to baseball on the White House lawn. "We boys hailed his coming with delight," one child recalled. "I remember vividly how he ran, how long were his strides, how far his coattails stuck out behind." In fact, Lincoln enjoyed playing so much that when visiting dignitaries interrupted him during a game, he said, "I am glad to hear of their coming, but they will have to wait a few minutes till I get my turn at bat."

Most presidents after Lincoln were just as enamored of the sport. Three—Andrew Johnson, Ulysses S. Grant, and Chester A. Arthur—formally welcomed organized baseball teams into the White House for visits. Benjamin Harrison became the first president to attend a Major League Baseball game while in office. The first recipient of a lifetime pass to Major League games was Theodore Roosevelt—a self-professed non-baseball fan who never once took advantage of the privilege.

On April 14, 1910, a new baseball tradition was born. Before a crowd of fifteen thousand, President William Howard Taft strode to the pitcher's mound at the center of Washington's American League Park, cupped a fresh white baseball in his right hand, and threw the first pitch of the season to Walter Johnson, pitcher for the Senators. Since that day, every president except Jimmy Carter has thrown at least one first pitch. Some pitches were thrown with skill, others with more enthusiasm than ability. But only one presidential first pitch has come to symbolize baseball's healing powers in the wake of tragedy.

Of all the presidents, George W. Bush may have the strongest ties with baseball. His uncle, Herbert Walker, was one of the original owners of the New York Mets. His father, former president George Bush, played baseball while at Yale University. George W. grew up playing Little League and was once part-owner of the Texas Rangers. Early on in his presidency, he opened the South Lawn of the White House to young T-ball players. "I never dreamed about being president," he has been quoted as saying. "I wanted to be Willie Mays."

Bush had been in the White House for less than a year when the tragic events of September 11, 2001, occurred. People worldwide reeled at the devastation and death caused by the terrorist attacks. The normal activities of daily life ground to a halt. Many professional sports, including baseball, canceled or postponed games until further notice.

One week after the tragedy, Major League Baseball responded to public and player appeals and resumed its season. While rescue and relief workers struggled at Ground Zero in Manhattan, the New York Yankees battled their way to pennant victory in the Bronx. Across the country, the Arizona Diamondbacks took the National League title to earn their first trip to the World Series. Games One and Two were played in Arizona and won by the home team. Then the Series moved to New York for Game Three.

A month and a half after the terrorist attacks, New Yorkers were still learning to cope with the tragedy that had struck at the heart of their city. For many, the upcoming match was a welcome chance to focus on something positive. A home-game victory by their beloved Yankees would give them a boost like nothing else.

President Bush recognized how important this game was to the morale of New Yorkers, and to the world. On October 30, amid massive security and circling fighter planes, Bush took the mound in Yankee Stadium. Wearing a sweatshirt emblazoned with the initials *FDNY* in honor of the New York City Fire Department, he gave a thumbs-up signal to a sellout crowd of more than 57,000 fans. Then he reared back and threw the first pitch, a perfect strike just off-center of the plate, to Yankees catcher Todd Greene.

The Yankees went on to win that third game, although they eventually lost the Series to the powerhouse Diamondbacks. The Series had been a well-fought battle, memorable not only because of the great plays made and home runs batted, but because it proved to the world that although the United States had been battered, it was not beaten. The events of 9/11 will never be erased, but that presidential pitch, the first thrown since the attacks, spoke volumes about America's resilience in the face of tragedy.

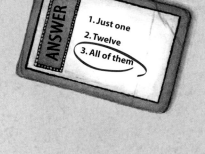

ANSWER

1. Just one
2. Twelve
3. All of them

Wanted: Magnanimous, Exquisite Woman!

dialogue between Gigi Amateau and her daughter, Judith, age 13

MOM: So, Judith, should we have a woman president in the White House?

JUDITH: We should. We've had, what, forty-three presidents? And they've all been men. That's boring.

M: England elected a woman prime minister, like, twenty-five years ago, or thirty—a long time ago, anyway.

J: Really? We're behind.

M: Well, what's it going to take?

J: Women just have to get out there and run, like they are now.

M: Women have run in the past.

J: They have?

M: Sure. Pat Schroeder ran. So did Carol Moseley Braun and Elizabeth Dole. And more. But no woman has ever won her party's nomination.

J: Right. Well, that's what I meant, Mom.

M: A woman got the nomination for vice president once.

J: Really? Cool. Who was that?

M: Geraldine Ferraro. She was from New York.

J: See? They don't even teach about her.

A woman just needs to step up and do it, no matter what anyone else says. She needs to not let anyone talk her out of it and not listen to anyone who says "You can't" or "You shouldn't." She should just say, "I'm going to run for president," and be mag-mag-magnanimous! See? I remembered that word.

M: *Magnanimous,* good word. What does it mean?

J: To be bigger than the negativity. We need a woman who will be magnanimous and say, "I'm not going to be a mudslinger. I'm going to show you who I am."

M: That's deep. That's deeper than history.

J: Mom, nothing is deeper than history. Not even the ocean.

M: So, who would make a good woman president?

J: Eleanor Roosevelt would have been a great president.

M: Go, Eleanor. Who else would be good for the job?

J: I would be a good president. Don't you think so?

M: Absolutely.

J: Why do you think I'd make a good president?

M: Well, I can think of a lot of reasons. You have a keen mind, and you also have a big heart. You analyze each situation before you act. I've never known you to hurt someone just to see them hurt. You consider the feelings and needs of those around you. You try to find ways for people to save face when necessary. You're sort of a conformist, yet you're not afraid to state your case and go your own way. You love children, the earth, and old people. You love America. You got that from me, by the way. Who taught you to sing "The Star-Spangled Banner" when you were little?

J: Gram.

M: She did not! I taught you the national anthem—that's my patriotic song. Maybe Gram taught you "This Land Is Your Land."

J: OK, we'll go with that. Hey, Mom? I'm going to change my thinking from what it has been so far.

M: Go for it, Judith.

J: I wouldn't want a woman to be president just because she is a woman. In a way, that would be dissing women. I mean a woman should have been elected president a long time ago. But we should only vote for a woman to be president if we agree with her views and if she would do a good job.

M: I'm with you. So let's write a poem about all this.

J: Do we have to?

M: Yes! It'll be fun. We'll play a game called the Exquisite Corpse.

J: "Corpse?" As in a dead body? That sounds scary!

M: Sweetie, the game isn't scary. *Corpse* just means the end result is patched together from different parts—yours and mine. All right, it's sort of like how Frankenstein was made, but with words. I'll write a line and then fold the paper over so you can't see what I wrote. You write a line, then cover up what you wrote. Then I will. Then you will, and on and on until we decide to stop.

J: What if it doesn't make sense?

M: Well, then, it just doesn't. The fun part is seeing what we've got when we blend our thoughts together.

It must be lonely in there,
Where everything flows from one
         fundamental hope, not a law.

Caring enough to thrash young men who
         would blow smoke in your face,
Standing in front, not seeing a single
         flaw ahead of you.

Who hears your whispers?

You've stood for so many
         and housed so many.

Which to hold?
I wonder about the ones not yet arrived.

Mrs. Bush Inspires a National Book Festival

JOHN Y. COLE

POSTER BY CAROL DYER

THE IDEA OF A NATIONAL BOOK FESTIVAL came from First Lady Laura Bush. A former schoolteacher and librarian, Mrs. Bush established the Texas Book Festival when she was First Lady of that state. After George W. Bush was elected president of the United States, Mrs. Bush invited Librarian of Congress James H. Billington and the Library of Congress to join her in creating and hosting the National Book Festival.

The Festival celebrates the joys of reading by attracting popular and award-winning authors who appeal to a wide variety of children and adults. It is a family event, open to the public and free. It focuses on author presentations and book signings, giving members of the public the opportunity to meet and be inspired by their favorite writers and illustrators. All of the presentations and book signings take place on a single day. It is nonpartisan and noncommercial, supported entirely by private donations solicited by the Library of

Congress. Publishers are invited to nominate nationally known authors, illustrators, or poets to participate in the event.

On September 8, 2001, three days before the terrorist attacks on the World Trade Center and the Pentagon, First Lady Laura Bush and the Library of Congress hosted the first National Book Festival. On this warm and sunny day, approximately 25,000 members of the public came to Capitol Hill to enjoy hearing more than sixty authors, illustrators, and poets talk about and sign their latest books. A storybook atmosphere prevailed in the Library's Jefferson and Madison Buildings and on the east Capitol grounds.

In the aftermath of September 11, the future of the National Book Festival was uncertain. Leonard Kniffel, the editor of *American Libraries,* caught the mood in an editorial titled "The Beginning of a Great Festival Suddenly Seems Like an Ending." This unique (and delicate) partnership between the executive and legislative arms of the American government easily could have been lost in the government's need to react first and foremost to the events of September 11.

However, Mrs. Bush never wavered in her determination to proceed, and the Library of Congress was in full agreement. The 2002 National Book Festival was held outdoors on the west Capitol grounds and the National Mall. In addition to the author-presentation pavilions, it offered two reading-promotion pavilions and a Pavilion of the States, in which each state, plus the District of Columbia and four U.S. territories, shared information about statewide author-, reading-, and library-promotion programs. In spite of poor weather and an ongoing sniper threat in the Washington, D.C., area, the festival attracted a crowd of 45,000, and its place as an annual event seemed assured. The 2003 festival moved to the National Mall, and nearly 70,000 people attended, enjoying their favorite writers and a new poetry pavilion.

The 2004 festival was hosted by First Lady Laura Bush and featured seventy-six authors, illustrators, and poets, and a new pavilion: Science Fiction & Fantasy. Drawing its largest crowd yet, approximately 85,000 book lovers turned out for the fourth annual National Book Festival.

In 2005 fiction and science fiction were combined into a new Fiction and Fantasy Pavilion, featuring authors and illustrators of books for both children and teens, and continued to be enormously popular. Festival attendance soared to 100,000 in 2005, stayed at the same level in 2006, and reached 120,000 in 2007. Furthermore, in these years the festival stretched to its full and current size of seven city blocks (from 7th to 14th Streets) on America's National Mall.

The National Book Festival is building a unique historical record; most of the presentations by authors, illustrators, poets, and storytellers at the first six National Book Festivals (2001–2006) can been seen and heard on the Library of Congress's website.

1600 PENNSYLVANIA AVE.

WHO'S IN THE HOUSE?

1600 PENNSYLVANIA AVE.
CREATED BY
BOB KOLAR

NICE PLACE
WE'VE GOT
HERE.

TODAY
ONLY
BARGAINS

SEND

11 12 13 14 15 16 17 18 19 20 21 22 23 24

38 39 40 41 42 43 44 ?

1600 PENNSYLVANIA AVE.

1. **George Washington, 1789–1797**
George Washington never lived in the White House, but he helped pick out the site.

2. **John Adams, 1797–1801**
John Adams was the first president to move into the White House.

3. **Thomas Jefferson, 1801–1809**
President Jefferson had indoor bathrooms added to the White House.

4. **James Madison, 1809–1817**
During President Madison's stay, the White House was burned and ransacked by the British.

5. **James Monroe, 1817–1825**
President Monroe got into financial hardships because of his extravagant White House decorating.

6. **John Quincy Adams, 1825–1829**
John Quincy Adams loved gardening and expanded the White House gardens.

7. **Andrew Jackson, 1829–1837**
President Jackson was the first to enjoy running water at the White House.

8. **Martin Van Buren, 1837–1841**
President Van Buren kept toasty warm with the new heating system added to the White House.

9. **William Henry Harrison, 1841**
On the day President Harrison moved into the White House, he made an inaugural speech that was almost two hours long.

10. **John Tyler, 1841–1845**
John Tyler oversaw a very busy White House. He had fifteen children.

11. **James K. Polk, 1845–1849**
Hardworking President Polk never took a vacation away from the White House.

12. **Zachary Taylor, 1849–1850**
Zachary Taylor was the first career soldier to live in the White House.

13. **Millard Fillmore, 1850–1853**
President Fillmore and his wife, Abigail, established the first library in the White House.

14. **Franklin Pierce, 1853–1857**
Franklin Pierce added a bathroom to the second-floor living quarters of the White House. It was quite luxurious, with hot and cold running water.

15. **James Buchanan, 1857–1861**
Since President Buchanan was not married, his niece came to the White House to serve as his hostess.

16. **Abraham Lincoln, 1861–1865**
At six feet four inches, President Lincoln was the tallest resident of the White House. The Lincoln Bedroom is the only room in the White House named after a president.

17. **Andrew Johnson, 1865–1869**
During Andrew Johnson's presidency, cows were kept on the White House grounds to provide fresh milk to the first family.

18. **Ulysses S. Grant, 1869–1877**
The White House of Ulysses S. Grant had the reputation of being a party place.

19. Rutherford B. Hayes, 1877–1881
Rutherford B. Hayes liked to spend his White House evenings singing hymns with his family and friends.

20. James A. Garfield, 1881
James A. Garfield was shot and was on his White House deathbed for eighty days.

21. Chester A. Arthur, 1881–1885
Chester A. Arthur held a yard sale at the White House.

22. Grover Cleveland, 1885–1889
Grover Cleveland's oldest daughter, Ruth, was one of the most popular White House kids. The Baby Ruth candy bar was named after her.

23. Benjamin Harrison, 1889–1893
Benjamin Harrison was the last president to have a beard and the first to have electric lighting in the White House.

24. Grover Cleveland, 1893–1897
Esther, another of Grover Cleveland's daughters, was the only president's child ever born at the White House.

25. William McKinley, 1897–1901
William McKinley's wife, Ida, spent much of her White House years knitting booties — some 3,500 pairs in all.

26. Theodore Roosevelt, 1901–1909
Theodore Roosevelt, true to his adventuresome ways, was the first president to ride in a car, fly in a plane, and dive in a submarine, and he oversaw a major restoration of the White House.

27. William H. Taft, 1909–1913
William H. Taft was a big guy — so big that he had to have jumbo bathtubs installed in the White House.

28. Woodrow Wilson, 1913–1921
Woodrow Wilson placed the first transcontinental phone call from the Oval Office.

29. Warren G. Harding, 1921–1923
President Harding had the first radio installed in the White House.

30. Calvin Coolidge, 1923–1929
Calvin Coolidge lit the first National Christmas Tree on the White House grounds.

31. Herbert C. Hoover, 1929–1933
Herbert Hoover had to rebuild the West Wing of the White House after a Christmas Eve fire.

32. Franklin D. Roosevelt, 1933–1945
Franklin D. Roosevelt was the first president to swim in the White House swimming pool.

33. Harry S. Truman, 1945–1953
President Truman invited television cameras on a tour of the White House.

34. Dwight D. Eisenhower, 1953–1961
Dwight D. Eisenhower was a World War II hero and a heck of a golfer. He had a putting green built on the White House grounds.

35. John F. Kennedy, 1961–1963
President Kennedy wanted to send an American to the moon but also took care of things around the White House. He had the Rose Garden rebuilt.

36. Lyndon B. Johnson, 1963–1969
Lyndon B. Johnson installed telephones in the White House bathrooms so that he could be in touch at all times.

37. Richard M. Nixon, 1969–1974
President Nixon had new uniforms made for the White House police force. They looked silly, however, and were later given to a high-school marching band in Iowa.

38. Gerald R. Ford, 1974–1977
President Ford locked himself out of the White House one night while walking his dog.

39. Jimmy Carter, 1977–1981
President Jimmy Carter had the first computers installed in the White House.

40. Ronald Reagan, 1981–1989
While President Reagan was in office, the White House had a little makeover, including a fancy new set of dishes.

41. George H. W. Bush, 1989–1993
President Bush sent the first e-mail from the White House and banned broccoli from White House menus.

42. William J. Clinton, 1993–2001
President Clinton enjoyed White House free time by making some smooth music on his saxophone.

43. George W. Bush, 2001–2008
Presidents Bush and Bush are the second father-and-son team to live in the White House, following presidents Adams and Adams.

44. Fill in the blank!

The White House by Moonlight

Walt Whitman (1819–1892)

illustrated by **James Ransome**

February 24th.—A spell of fine soft weather. I wander about a good deal, sometimes at night under the moon. To-night took a long look at the President's house. The white portico—the palace-like, tall, round columns, spotless as snow—the walls also—the tender and soft moonlight, flooding the pale marble, and making peculiar faint languishing shades, not shadows—everywhere a soft transparent hazy, thin, blue moon-lace, hanging in the air—the brilliant and extra-plentiful clusters of gas, on and around the façade, columns, portico, &c.—everything so white, so marbly pure and dazzling, yet soft—the White House of future poems, and of dreams and dramas, there in the soft and copious moon—the gorgeous front, in the trees, under the lustrous flooding moon, full of reality, full of illusion—the forms of the trees, leafless, silent, in trunk and myriad-angles of branches, under the stars and sky—the White House of the land, and of beauty and night—sentries at the gates, and by the portico, silent, pacing there in blue overcoats—stopping you not at all, but eyeing you with sharp eyes, whichever way you move.

Dear Readers,

THE NATIONAL CHILDREN'S BOOK AND LITERACY ALLIANCE created *Our White House: Looking In, Looking Out,* a book of America's stories for young people to read and share with their families, friends, teachers, and classmates. The seed that grew to become *Our White House* was planted by NCBLA honorary board member David McCullough, who made us aware of the profound connection between literacy and historical literacy by expressing his belief that great storytelling and art can get young people excited about history. We hope *Our White House* will tempt you to investigate the history, literature, and art that make America's heritage rich, diverse, and endlessly fascinating.

The NCBLA, a not-for-profit organization founded by award-winning authors and illustrators of books for children and young adults, advocates for and educates about literacy, literature, libraries, and the arts. We believe that literacy is essential to the development of responsible citizens in a democracy and that all young people must have equal access to exciting and interesting books and information sources that invite them to dream and give them the tools to achieve their dreams. As writers and illustrators, teachers and mentors, parents, grandparents, aunts, and uncles, our ultimate question is always, How can we best serve all our nation's children? The gifted contributors to *Our White House* have donated their time and talent because they, too, believe that literacy is about much more than the ability to read.

President John Adams, the first occupant of the White House, wrote,

> *Liberty cannot be preserved without a general knowledge among the people, who have a right . . . to knowledge . . . and a desire to know; but besides this, they have a right, an indisputable, unalienable, indefeasible, divine right to that most dreaded and envied kind of knowledge, I mean, of the characters and conduct of their rulers.*

We hope that sharing *Our White House* with family and friends will be the first step toward acquiring that vital knowledge.

Thank you,
The National Children's Book and Literacy Alliance

NOTES ON SOURCES USED BY THE AUTHORS

pp. 4–10: Based on historical fact, the "Testimony of Padraig Tomás Ó'Deoráin: 1801" is a fictionalized account of an Irish apprentice stonecutter's experience.

pp. 20–21: The poem "On the Discoveries of Captain Lewis" can be found in Richard Dillon, *Meriwether Lewis: A Biography* (New York: Coward-McCann, 1965), pp. 274–278.

pp. 34–35: Based on historical fact, "The Burning of the White House" is a fictional letter.

pp. 36–38: "Dolley Madison Rescues George Washington" is based on the following:

Anthony, Katharine. *Dolly Madison: Her Life and Times.* Garden City, NY: Doubleday, 1949.

Flanagan, Alice K. *Dolley Payne Todd Madison, 1768–1849.* New York: Children's Press, 1997.

Jensen, Amy La Follette. *The White House and Its Thirty-Four Families.* New York: McGraw Hill, 1965.

Madison, Dolley. *Memoirs and Letters of Dolley Madison.* Boston: Houghton Mifflin, 1886.

pp. 57–59: "Andy and Me" is based on *Sketches and Eccentricities of Col. David Crockett of West Tennessee* (New York: Harper, 1833), p. 164.

pp. 70–72: "Elizabeth Keckly: Seamstress to First Lady Mary Todd Lincoln, 1861–1865" is based on the following:

Fleischner, Jennifer. *Mrs. Lincoln and Mrs. Keckly: The Remarkable Story of a Friendship Between a First Lady and a Former Slave.* New York: Broadway Books, 2003.

Keckly, Elizabeth. *Behind the Scenes, or, Thirty Years a Slave and Four Years in the White House.* New York: Carleton, 1868, and New York: Penguin, 2005.

pp. 74–75: "High Spirits in the Lincoln White House" is based on the following:

Thomas, Benjamin P. *Abraham Lincoln.* New York: Knopf, 1952, p. 302.

Ward, Geoffrey C. *Lincoln and His Family,* a pamphlet published as part of the project "Lincoln's Thought and the Present." Springfield, IL: Sangamon State University, 1978, p. 21.

pp. 89–92: "The Eyes and Ears of the Public" is based on the following:

Ames, Mary Clemmer. *Ten Years in Washington: Life and Scenes in the National Capital as a Woman Sees Them.* Hartford, CT: Worthington, 1874, p. 254.

Thomas, Helen. *Front Row at the White House: My Life and Times.* New York: Scribner, 1999, pp. 100 and 124.

pp. 93–95, 98–99: "Theodore Roosevelt's Letters to His Children" and "Storming Down the Stairs" are based on the following:

Bishop, Joseph Bucklin, ed. *Theodore Roosevelt's Letters to His Children.* New York: Scribner, 1919.

Kerr, Joan Patterson, ed. *A Bully Father: Theodore Roosevelt's Letters to His Children.* New York: Random House, 1995.

Morris, Edmund. *Theodore Rex.* New York: Random House, 2001.

pp. 116–119: "Hoover's One Term" is based on the following:

Ellis, Edward Robb. *A Nation in Torment: The Great American Depression, 1929–1939.* New York: Coward-McCann, 1970, and New York: Kodansha, 1995.

Herbert Hoover Presidential Library & Museum website. http://www.hoover.archives.gov/

Hoover, Herbert. *The Memoirs of Herbert Hoover: The Great Depression, 1929–1941.* New York: Macmillan, 1952, p. 195.

The White House website. http://www.whitehouse.gov/history/presidents/hh31.html

pp. 132–137: "Hands" is based on Douglas Chandor, *Portrait of Eleanor Roosevelt* (New York, 1949), a painting exhibited in the Vermeil Room at the White House, and on David B. Roosevelt and Manuela Dunn-Mascetti, *Grandmère: A Personal History of Eleanor Roosevelt* (New York: Warner Books, 2002).

pp. 212–214: Letters included in "The Green House" are fictionalized.

COPYRIGHT ACKNOWLEDGMENTS AND CREDITS FOR PUBLIC DOMAIN MATERIALS

CONTRIBUTORS TO *OUR WHITE HOUSE*

Stephen Alcorn is the illustrator of *Let It Shine*, winner of the Carter G. Woodson Book Award, and *My America: A Poetry Atlas of the United States*, a *Children's Literature* Choice List Title.

Gigi Amateau is the author of *Claiming Georgia Tate*, which was nominated as a New York Public Library Book for the Teen Age.

M. T. Anderson is the author of *Feed*, a National Book Award Finalist and a *Los Angeles Times* Book Prize Finalist, as well as the National Book Award Winner and Michael L. Printz Honor Book *The Astonishing Life of Octavian Nothing, Traitor to the Nation, Volume 1: The Pox Party*. He is a member of the board of directors of the NCBLA.

Jennifer Armstrong is the author of *Shipwreck at the Bottom of the World: The Extraordinary True Story of Shackleton and the* Endurance, which was awarded a *Boston Globe–Horn Book* Honor in nonfiction, as well as *Photo by Brady: A Picture of the Civil War*, a James Madison Honor Book.

Jeannine Atkins is the author of *A Name on the Quilt*, an *American Bookseller* "Pick of the Lists" Selection, as well as *Aani and the Tree Huggers*, which was nominated as a *Smithsonian* Notable Book for Children.

Tony Auth is a Pulitzer Prize–winning editorial cartoonist for the *Philadelphia Inquirer*. He is also the illustrator of *Topsy-Turvy Bedtime*.

Natalie Babbitt is the author of *Tuck Everlasting*, an American Library Association Notable Children's Book, and Newbery Honor Book *Knee-Knock Rise*. She is a member of the board of directors of the NCBLA.

Mary Brigid Barrett is the author of *Sing to the Stars*, an *American Bookseller* "Pick of the Lists" Selection, and author-illustrator of *The Man of the House at Huffington Row: A Christmas Story*. She is the founder, president, and executive director of the NCBLA.

Sophie Blackall is the illustrator of *Ruby's Wish*, winner of the Ezra Jack Keats New Illustrator Award, and *Red Butterfly: How a Princess Smuggled the Secret of Silk Out of China*.

Jess M. Brallier is the author of *Who Was Albert Einstein?* and *Lawyers and Other Reptiles*.

Calef Brown is the illustrator of *The Neddiad* and *Flamingos on the Roof*.

Don Brown is the author and illustrator of *Dolley Madison Saves George Washington* and *Across a Dark and Wild Sea*.

Joseph Bruchac is the author of *Code Talker: A Novel About the Navajo Marines of World War Two* and *Thirteen Moons on Turtle's Back*. He is the winner of a Lifetime Achievement Award from the Native Writers' Circle of the Americas.

Robert Byrd is the illustrator of *Leonardo: Beautiful Dreamer*, winner of a Golden Kite Award, and of *The Hero Schliemann: The Dreamer Who Dug for Troy*.

Meg Cabot is the author of the Princess Diaries series, the first of which was an American Library Association Best Book for Young Adults, and the Heather Wells Mystery series.

Eric Carle is the illustrator of numerous award-winning books, including *The Very Hungry Caterpillar*, and is the co-founder of the Eric Carle Museum of Picture Book Art.

Nancy Carpenter is the illustrator of *Apples to Oregon*, an American Library Association Notable Children's Book, and *Sitti's Secrets*, winner of a Jane Addams Picture Book Award.

Joe Cepeda is the illustrator of *What a Truly Cool World*, one of *Family Life* Magazine's Top Ten Best Books of the Year, and *Mice and Beans*, a *Child* Magazine Best Book of the Year.

R. Gregory Christie is the illustrator of *Only Passing Through: The Story of Sojourner Truth* and *Brothers in Hope: The Story of the Lost Boys of Sudan*, both Coretta Scott King Illustrator Award Honor Books.

John Y. Cole is a librarian and historian who serves as the director of the Library of Congress's Center for the Book, an organization that aims to stimulate public interest in books and reading and to encourage the historical study of books and their influence.

Michael L. Cooper is the author of the Golden Kite Award winner *Dust to Eat: Drought and Depression in the 1930s* as well as *Fighting for Honor: Japanese Americans and World War II*, which was nominated as a New York Public Library Book for the Teen Age.

Susan Cooper is the author of the award-winning Dark Is Rising series, including *The Dark Is Rising*, a Newbery Honor Book, and *The Grey King*, a Newbery Medal winner. She is a member of the board of directors of the NCBLA.

Marguerite W. Davol is the author of *The Paper Dragon*, an American Library Association Notable Children's Book, as well as *Black, White, Just Right!*

Kate DiCamillo is the author of the Newbery Honor Book *Because of Winn-Dixie*, as well as *The Tale of Despereaux: Being the Story of a Mouse, a Princess, Some Soup, and a Spool of Thread*, which won the Newbery Medal.

Leo and Diane Dillon are the illustrator team of *Why Mosquitoes Buzz in People's Ears* and *Ashanti to Zulu: African Traditions*, both winners of the Caldecott Medal.

Carol Dyer is a painter and printmaker who specializes in an American folk-art style. She provided paintings for *Album of American Traditions*.

Jane Dyer is the illustrator of *Move Over, Rover!*, a Theodore Seuss Geisel Honor Book, and *Time for Bed*.

Timothy Basil Ering is the illustrator of *The Tale of Despereaux: Being the Story of a Mouse, a Princess, Some Soup, and a Spool of Thread*, winner of the Newbery Medal, and the author-illustrator of *The Story of Frog Belly Rat Bone*.

Russell Freedman is the author of *The Voice That Challenged a Nation: Marian Anderson and the Struggle for Equal Rights*, which received a Newbery Honor, as well as *Lincoln: A Photobiography*, a Newbery Medal winner.

Tony Fucile was the supervising animator for the Oscar-winning films *Finding Nemo* and *The Incredibles*.

Jean Craighead George is the author of the Newbery Medal winner *Julie of the Wolves* as well as the Newbery Honor Book *My Side of the Mountain*.

Leonid Gore is the illustrator of *Jacob and the Stranger*, winner of an Anne Izard Storytellers' Choice Award, and *Behold the Trees*, a Book Sense 76 Selection.

Max Grafe is the illustrator of *Old Coyote*, a Book Sense 76 Selection, and *The Bearskinner*.

Barbara Harrison is the author of *Theo* and co-author of *Origins of Story: On Writing for Children*.

Kevin Hawkes is the illustrator of *Library Lion*, a *New York Times* bestseller, and *Weslandia*, a *Parenting* Reading Magic Award winner.

Homer Hickam is the author of *Rocket Boys* (also published as *October Sky*), which was a #1 *New York Times* bestseller, and the Josh Thurlow series.

Lee Bennett Hopkins is the editor of numerous poetry anthologies and the author of *Marvelous Math* and *My America: A Poetry Atlas of the United States*.

Polly Horvath is the author of *The Canning Season*, winner of the National Book Award, and *Everything on a Waffle*, a Newbery Honor Book.

Bagram Ibatoulline is the illustrator of *The Miraculous Journey of Edward Tulane*, a Boston Globe–Horn Book Award winner, and *The Nightingale*, an Oppenheim Toy Portfolio Platinum Award winner.

Paul B. Janeczko is the editor of many poetry anthologies, including *A Poke in the I: A Collection of Concrete Poems*, named a *New York Times Book Review* Best Illustrated Children's Book of the Year, and the author of *Top Secret: A Handbook of Codes, Ciphers, and Secret Writing*.

Steve Johnson and Lou Fancher are the illustrator team of *My Many Colored Days* by Dr. Seuss and *The Ugly Duckling* by Hans Christian Andersen.

Stéphane Jorisch is the illustrator of *Jabberwocky*, winner of a Governor General's Award, and *Footwork: The Story of Fred and Adele Astaire*.

Steven Kellogg is the illustrator of more than one hundred children's books, including *Is Your Mama a Llama?* and the Pinkerton series. He is a recipient of the Regina Medal and is a vice president of the board of directors of the NCBLA.

Barbara Kerley is the author of *The Dinosaurs of Waterhouse Hawkins*, a Caldecott Honor Book, as well as *What To Do About Alice?*

Ralph Ketcham is a professor of history emeritus at Syracuse University. He is the editor of *The Autobiography of Benjamin Franklin* and author of *The Idea of Democracy in the Modern Era*.

Elizabeth Cody Kimmel is the author of *My Penguin Osbert* and the Lily B. series.

Bob Kolar is the author-illustrator of *Racer Dogs* and the illustrator of *AlphaOops!*, a National Council of Teachers of English Notable Children's Book in the Language Arts.

Kathleen Krull is the author of the Lives of . . . biography series, as well as *Wilma Unlimited*, which was awarded a Jane Addams Picture Book Award.

Jim LaMarche is the illustrator of *The Carousel*, a *Parents* Best Book of the Year, and *The Raft*, an International Reading Association Teachers' Choice.

Stephanie Loer is a children's book critic who has been reviewing children's literature for more than twenty years. She is a member of the board of directors of the NCBLA.

William Low is the author-illustrator of *Old Penn Station* and *Chinatown* and the winner of four Silver Medals from the Society of Illustrators.

P.J. Lynch is the illustrator of *The Christmas Miracle of Jonathan Toomey*, winner of a Christopher Award, and *When Jessie Came Across the Sea*, an International Reading Association Notable Book for a Global Society.

David Macaulay is the author-illustrator of *Black and White*, winner of a Caldecott Medal, and of *The Way Things Work*, a *New York Times* bestseller. He is a member of the board of directors of the NCBLA.

Patricia MacLachlan is the author of *Sarah, Plain and Tall*, a Newbery Medal winner, and *Arthur, for the Very First Time*, a Golden Kite Award winner. She is a recipient of the National Humanities Medal and a member of the board of directors of the NCBLA.

Gregory Maguire is the author of novels for both adults and children, including *Wicked: The Life and Times of the Wicked Witch of the West*, which has been made into a hit Broadway musical, and *What-the-Dickens: The Story of a Rogue Tooth Fairy*, a *New York Times* bestseller. He is a member of the board of directors of the NCBLA.

Leonard S. Marcus is a literary critic and historian as well as an author and editor. He compiled and edited *The Wand in the Word: Conversations with Writers of Fantasy*, a *School Library Journal* Best Book of the Year, and edited *Lifelines: A Poetry Anthology Patterned on the Stages of Life*, which was a *Publishers Weekly* Best Children's Book of the Year.

Albert Marrin is a historian and author of *Old Hickory: Andrew Jackson and the American People*, a James Madison Book Award winner, and *Tatan'ka Iyota'ke: Sitting Bull and His World*.

Petra Mathers is the author-illustrator of the *Boston Globe–Horn Book* Honor winner *Sophie and Lou* and of *Lottie's New Friend*, a *New York Times Book Review* Best Illustrated Children's Book of the Year.

David McCullough is the author of *John Adams* and *Truman*, both winners of the Pulitzer Prize. He also won the National Book Award for both *The Path Between the Seas* and *Mornings on Horseback*.

Emily Arnold McCully is the author-illustrator of *Mirette on the High Wire*, winner of a Caldecott Medal, and *The Pirate Queen*.

Megan McDonald is the author of the *New York Times* best-selling Judy Moody series and the Stink series.

Patricia C. and Fredrick L. McKissack have co-authored more than one hundred books together. They are two-time winners of the Coretta Scott King Author Award. Their titles include *A Long Hard Journey: The Story of the Pullman Porter* and *Days of Jubilee*. Patricia is also the author of *The Dark-Thirty: Southern Tales of the Supernatural*, a Newbery Honor Book. They both serve on the board of directors of the NCBLA.

Meet the Press with Tim Russert is a weekly television news show that focuses on interviews with national leaders about the economy, foreign policy, and politics.

Milton Meltzer is the author of more than eighty books, including *Ten Queens: Portraits of Women of Power* and the Milton Meltzer Biographies series. He has been nominated for the National Book Award five times.

Wendell Minor is the illustrator of *Fire Storm*, winner of an Oppenheim Toy Portfolio Gold Award, and *Ghost Ship*, a *New York Times* bestseller.

Barry Moser is the illustrator of hundreds of books for children and adults, including *Alice's Adventures in Wonderland*, winner of the National Book Award for design and illustration, and *Moses*.

Roxie Munro is the author-illustrator of the Inside-Outside series and *Mazescapes*, a *Parenting* Pick of the Month.

Walter Dean Myers is the author of *Scorpions* and *Somewhere in the Darkness*, both Newbery Honor Books, as well as *Monster*, a National Book Award Finalist.

Claire Nivola is the author-illustrator of *Elisabeth* and the illustrator of *The Flag Maker*.

Linda Sue Park is the author of *A Single Shard*, a Newbery Medal winner, and *When My Name Was Keoko*. She is a member of the board of directors of the NCBLA.

Katherine Paterson is the author of *Bridge to Terabithia* and *Jacob Have I Loved*, both winners of the Newbery Medal. She has won the National Book Award twice. She is a vice president of the board of directors of the NCBLA.

Richard Peck is the author of *A Year Down Yonder*, a Newbery Medal winner, and *The Teacher's Funeral: A Comedy in Three Parts*, which received a Christopher Award.

Stephanie True Peters is the author of *A Princess Primer*, a *New York Times* bestseller, and co-author of *My First Nutcracker*.

Matt Phelan is the illustrator of *The Higher Power of Lucky*, a Newbery Medal winner, and *The New Girl*, a Parents' Choice Silver Honor winner.

Jerry Pinkney is the illustrator of *The Talking Eggs* and *Noah's Ark*, both Caldecott Honor Books, and *The Patchwork Quilt*, winner of a Coretta Scott King Illustrator Award.

Tom Pohrt is the author-illustrator of *Having a Wonderful Time*, winner of a Parents' Choice Silver Honor, and the illustrator of *Crow and Weasel*.

Don Powers is the illustrator of *The Silver Donkey*.

Jack Prelutsky is the first Children's Poet Laureate appointed by the Poetry Foundation. He is the author of *Something Big Has Been Here* and *Behold the Bold Umbrellaphant: And Other Poems*.

James Ransome is the illustrator of *The Creation*, winner of a Coretta Scott King Illustrator Award and an International Board on Books for Young People Honor Selection, and *This Is the Dream*.

Chris Raschka is the illustrator of *The Hello, Goodbye Window*, winner of a Caldecott Medal, and *Yo! Yes?*, a Caldecott Honor Book.

Mike Reagan is a map illustrator and graphic designer.

Lynda Johnson Robb is the oldest daughter of former president Lyndon B. Johnson and Lady Bird Johnson. She is the president of the National Home Library Foundation and chair emerita of Reading Is Fundamental.

Barry Root is the illustrator of *Someplace Else*, a *New York Times Book Review* Best Illustrated Children's Book of the Year, and *Gameday*, a Christopher Award winner.

S. D. Schindler is the illustrator of *Whittington*, a Newbery Honor Book, and *Terrible Storm*.

Jon Scieszka is the author of the Time Warp Trio series, as well as *The Stinky Cheese Man and Other Fairly Stupid Tales*, a Caldecott Honor Book.

Brian Selznick is the creator of *The Invention of Hugo Cabret*, a Caldecott Medal winner, and *The Dinosaurs of Waterhouse Hawkins*, a Caldecott Honor Book.

Chris Sheban is the illustrator of *I Met a Dinosaur* and *The Story of a Seagull and the Cat Who Taught Her to Fly*. His work has received both Gold and Silver Medals from the Society of Illustrators.

Anita Silvey has been both an editor and a book critic. She is currently a member of the board of directors of the Vermont Center for the Book. She is the author of *100 Best Books for Children* and editor of *The Essential Guide to Children's Books and Their Creators*.

Peter Sís is the winner of a MacArthur Fellowship and the illustrator of *Starry Messenger: Galileo Galilei*, a Caldecott Honor Book. Six of his books have been named *New York Times Book Review* Best Illustrated Children's Books of the Year.

David Slonim is the illustrator of *Moishe's Miracle*, a *New York Times Book Review* Best Illustrated Children's Book of the Year, and *He Came with the Couch*.

David Small is the illustrator of *The Gardener*, a Caldecott Honor Book, and *So You Want to Be President?*, winner of a Caldecott Medal.

Jerry Spinelli is the author of *Maniac Magee*, a Newbery Medal winner, and *Wringer*, a Newbery Honor Book.

Sarah Stewart is the author of *The Library*, a *New York Times Book Review* Notable Book of the Year, and *The Journey*, a *Smithsonian* Notable Book for Children.

Matt Tavares is the illustrator of *Oliver's Game*, winner of a Parents' Choice Silver Honor, and *Mudball*, winner of a Parents' Choice Gold Award.

Mark Teague is the illustrator of *How Do Dinosaurs Say Good Night?* and *Dear Mrs. LaRue: Letters from Obedience School*, both *New York Times* bestsellers.

Stephanie S. Tolan is the author of the Newbery Honor Book *Surviving the Applewhites* and the Christopher Award winner *Listen!*

Chris Van Dusen is the illustrator of *Mercy Watson Goes for a Ride*, a Theodor Seuss Geisel Award Honor Book, and the author-illustrator of *Down to the Sea with Mr. Magee*.

Diana Walker has won awards from the World Press, the White House News Photographers Association, and the National Press Photographers Association for her photographs of the presidents. She published a selection of them in *Public and Private: Twenty Years Photographing the Presidency*.

Andréa Wesson is the illustrator of *Opera Cat*, winner of an Oppenheim Toy Portfolio Gold Award, and the Evangeline Mudd books.

Terry Widener is the illustrator of *Lou Gehrig: The Luckiest Man*, a Boston Globe–Horn Book Honor winner, and *Joe Louis: America's Fighter*, a Society of Illustrators selection.

Nancy Willard is a poet and a writer of books for both adults and children, including *A Visit to William Blake's Inn: Poems for Innocent and Experienced Travelers*, which won the Newbery Medal and received a Caldecott Honor, and *The High Rise Glorious Skittle Skat Roarious Sky Pie Angel Food Cake*.

Mark London Williams is a journalist and teacher as well as the author of the Danger Boy series.

Michael Winerip is a Pulitzer Prize–winning reporter for the *New York Times* as well as the author of Junior Library Guild Selections *Adam Canfield of the Slash* and *Adam Canfield, Watch Your Back!*

Virginia Euwer Wolff is the author of *True Believer*, a National Book Award winner and Michael L. Printz Honor Book, and *Make Lemonade*, winner of a Golden Kite Award.

Jane Yolen is the author of *Owl Moon*, a Caldecott Medal winner, and the How Do Dinosaurs . . . ? series of picture books.

Ed Young is the author-illustrator of *Lon Po Po: A Red Riding Hood Story from China*, winner of a Caldecott Medal, and *Seven Blind Mice* and *The Emperor and the Kite*, both Caldecott Honor Books.

James Young, M.D., was the White House physician for both presidents Kennedy and Johnson during their terms in office.

INDEX

The White House Easter Egg Roll, 2003

The tradition of rolling Easter eggs on the White House lawn dates back more than 150 years. The first public Easter egg rolls were held outside the Capitol building, but in 1878 they were relocated to the South Lawn of the White House by then-president Rutherford B. Hayes. It is customary for the president, First Lady, any children or grandchildren, pets, and—of course—the Easter Bunny to attend the Egg Rolling, which is the White House's largest public celebration.

PAINTING BY
ERIC CARLE

This book has been many years in the making and is the creative collaboration of many talents: Karen Lotz, publisher and editor; Hilary Van Dusen and Kate Fletcher, editors; Chris Paul, art director and designer; Maryellen Hanley, Heather McGee, and James Weinberg, designers; Katie Kerr, art administrator; Gregg Hammerquist, graphic production director; Nathan Pyritz, typesetter; Amy Carlisle, managing editor; Alexandra Redmond, copy editor; Maggie Deslaurier, proofreader; Allison D'Andrea, production director; and Jim Mitchell, production controller.

A Big Chair to Fill
ILLUSTRATION BY
Leonid Gore